Law and Chance

Law and Chance

Emanuele Severino
Translated by
Damiano Sacco
Edited by Giulio Goggi,
Damiano Sacco,
Ines Testoni

BLOOMSBURY ACADEMIC
LONDON • NEW YORK • OXFORD • NEW DELHI • SYDNEY

BLOOMSBURY ACADEMIC
Bloomsbury Publishing Plc
50 Bedford Square, London, WC1B 3DP, UK
1385 Broadway, New York, NY 10018, USA
29 Earlsfort Terrace, Dublin 2, Ireland

BLOOMSBURY, BLOOMSBURY ACADEMIC and the Diana logo are
trademarks of Bloomsbury Publishing Plc

First published in 1979 in Italy as Legge e caso by Emanuele Severino ©
Adelphi Edizioni

First published in Great Britain 2023

English language translation © Damiano Sacco 2023

Copyright © Giulio Goggi, Damiano Sacco and Ines Testoni, 2023

Giulio Goggi, Damiano Sacco and Ines Testoni have asserted their right under the
Copyright, Designs and Patents Act, 1988, to be identified as Editors of this work.

This book has been translated thanks to a translation grant awarded by the Italian
Ministry of Foreign Affairs and International Cooperation.

Questo libro è stato tradotto grazie a un contributo alla traduzione assegnato dal
Ministero degli Affari Esteri e della Cooperazione Internazionale italiano.

Series design: Ben Anslow
Photograph: Emanuele Severino (© Armando Rotoletti)

Bloomsbury Publishing Plc does not have any control over, or responsibility for, any
third-party websites referred to or in this book. All internet addresses given in this
book were correct at the time of going to press. The author and publisher regret
any inconvenience caused if addresses have changed or sites have ceased to exist,
but can accept no responsibility for any such changes.

A catalogue record for this book is available from the British Library.

A catalog record for this book is available from the Library of Congress.

ISBN: HB: 978-1-3500-7312-2
        PB: 978-1-3500-7313-9
        ePDF: 978-1-3500-7314-6
        eBook: 978-1-3500-7315-3

Typeset by RefineCatch Limited, Bungay, Suffolk
Printed and bound in Great Britain

To find out more about our authors and books visit www.bloomsbury.com
and sign up for our newsletters.

Contents

Emanuele Severino: Beyond the Alienated Soul of Tradition and Contemporary Philosophical Thought viii
    Ines Testoni & Giulio Goggi
The Translation of Destiny, and the Destiny of Translation xxii
    Damiano Sacco

Note on the Text xl

Part One Law and Chance

The Immutables, Nothingness, Chance 3

From Epistemic to Scientific Domination 21

The Greek Meaning of Nothingness in Modern
    Science 31

The Will to Power as Interpretation 53

Part Two Notes on the Problem of
Intersubjectivity in R. Carnap's *The Logical
Structure of the World*

1   The Unity of Knowledge 63

2   Experience and the Intersubjectivity of
    Knowledge 67

3   The Protocol-Statement Debate 75

4   The Presupposition of Intersubjectivity in *The
    Logical Structure of the World* 79

5   Intersubjective Knowledge *qua* Structural
    Knowledge 85

6   Intersubjectivity and Objectivity 91

7   The Concept of Construction 99

8   Realist Language Formulation of the Concept of
    Construction 105

9   The Realist and Constructional Meaning of
    Intersubjectivity in the *Structure* 111

10 The Constructional Order According to Cognitive
    Primacy 119

11 Elementary Lived Experiences and the Reason for
    their Unanalysability 127

12 The Method of Quasi-Analysis: Goodman's Critical
Observations 133

13 Scientific-Ordinary Knowledge and Constructional
Systems 143

Notes 157

Index 165

Emanuele Severino: Beyond the Alienated Soul of Tradition and Contemporary Philosophical Thought

INES TESTONI & GIULIO GOGGI

Emanuele Severino (Brescia, 26 February 1929 – Brescia, 17 January 2020) was one of the most important contemporary Italian philosophers. Because of his radical opposition to the idea that being is subject to the tyranny of time, he is commonly defined simultaneously as an anti-traditional and anti-contemporary thinker.

But who is Emanuele Severino, and what kind of challenge does he pose to Western thought? His enterprise first began with a substantial separation from historical metaphysics and traditional thought, but in his entire opera he also expounded his abysmal distancing from neo-idealism, phenomenology, existentialism, logical empiricism, pragmatism, Marxism, any linguistic turn or any post-structuralist philosophy of the Anglophone, French and German schools. The first key concept of that incommensurable separation is the discourse that affirms that everything exists forever, and that everything is eternal in each moment. Every part of reality is, and is ad infinitum, since whatever is cannot come into being from nothingness, or cease to be by falling into nothingness; indeed, if the being of what is were generated or corrupted, it would not be – there would be a time when being is not. The scandal of becoming is this: that being is not! This means that every being – all people, animals, vegetables and atoms or all relationships, instants, experiences, states of consciousness and events – from the most irrelevant to the most significant, everything that 'appears' in any way is eternal. 'Eternal' means that it is necessary that each being be and be as it is. And it is impossible for any being not to be. Everything that is not nothing is a being. 'Appearing' means entering the horizon of experience.

The further key concept for which the distance from the entirety of philosophy becomes sidereal is the definition of 'nihilism' and of the 'nihilistic folly': any kind of reduction of being to a product of time is a nihilistic folly. Since nothing resides outside of being, beings cannot turn into nothingness, and nothing can really turn into being. Any faith that believes in the oscillation of beings between nothingness and being is a nihilistic folly. The history of thought, however, is nihilistic. The error lies in the claim that the appearing of 'becoming' in the world amounts to the appearing of the annihilation of beings that become. What nihilism is unable to conceive is that nothing can be annihilated, and when something disappears (and it is also the very appearing of what enters the horizon of appearing that disappears), it means that it is going beyond, crossing the threshold of what presently appears, declining towards the invisible land of what does not appear here. The nihilistic folly that characterises the entire history of thought considers beings that appear in this world as destined to their annihilation. Indeed, nihilism is unable to admit that what no longer appears stays and appears eternally in a further dimension of being.

The third axis on which the sidereal distance distinguishes Severino, especially from other contemporary philosophers, is his organic, unitary and structurally coherent system of thought, whose intrinsic cogency derives from his radical redefinition of the concept of truth. Actually, if rigorous thinking may sometimes appear less than captivating, Severino's texts are an exception: the stricter they are, the more interesting the results, because his indication of 'eternity' is not rooted in any religious faith or poetic intuition, but in a rigorous foundation that is shown through irrefutable and radically integrated sentences. The concept of truth that Severino proposes refers precisely to *the incontrovertible* that shows the self-contradictory and self-negating nature of what intends to deny the originarily true assertion.

When he was only twenty-two, Emanuele Severino obtained a lecturer position in theoretical philosophy, and soon became full professor in moral philosophy at the Catholic University of Milan, and later full professor of theoretical philosophy at the University of Venice. He was also a member of the prestigious

Accademia dei Lincei,[1] and he was nominated Cavaliere di Gran Croce by the president of the Italian Republic. The passage from the Catholic University to the University of Venice was due to the Former Saint Office's inquisition process that Severino underwent for his ideas on eternity, and for the confutation of any ontological difference, understood as the ontological dependence of the creature on the creator. Since the eternity of every being implies that everything that presently appears is a positivity included in the eternal totality of beings, the true ontological difference is the difference between being as it appears procedurally (and therefore does not appear in its being concretely enveloped by the Whole) and being as it appears in its concrete dwelling in the Whole – which implies that what presently appears (including the present appearing of being) is a moment of the immutable Whole. Precisely because of this foundation, his indication developed by deeply questioning the entire traditional and metaphysical meaning of knowledge and action. This reasoning recuperates the absolute primacy of philosophy, which cannot be made subordinate to any religion or be secondary to science. The concept of truth that Severino proposes refers precisely to the incontrovertible that shows the self-contradictory and self-negating nature of what intends to deny truth. What is incontrovertible is the appearing of the self-identical being (and therefore of the non-contradictory being) of any being, and it is this self-identical being of any being that implies the eternity of every being as being. The primacy of true philosophical discourse – over all the arguments that seek to impose a content on the basis of a faith by presenting it as true

– occurs through the *élenchos*, i.e. the argumentative dynamic
that shows the self-negation of a faith, thereby showing the
nothingness of the content which in that faith is (contradictorily)
believed to be a non-nothingness. However, according to
Severino, on this basis, it is necessary to affirm that the contents
of science are also based on a faith. Certainly, the two faiths
based on the content of religions and empirical experimentation,
respectively, are distinguished from each other. It is possible,
however, to say that they are both faiths because they share a
common fundamental trait: the faith in becoming, that is, the
belief (which the West has always regarded not as a faith but as
the fundamental self-evidence itself) that the beings that inhabit
experience oscillate between being and nothingness. One of
Severino's most interesting contributions is precisely his ability
to show how nihilism (the persuasion/belief that being is
nothing) operates in both traditional and contemporary thought
and science, highlighting the relationships between them.

The relationship between contemporary and traditional
philosophy is the fourth significant trait of differentiation from
any other thought. Taking an epistemological slant, *Law and
Chance* is part of the critical analysis of this relationship. This
volume was published in 1979 after works of fundamental
importance – including *The Originary Structure* (*La struttura
originaria*) and *The Essence of Nihilism* (*Essenza del nichilismo*)
– had substantiated the foundation of Severino's discourse.[2] In
this book, the reason for the domination of science and
technology is considered and related to the whole history of
philosophy, particularly the origin of Greek thought. The analysis

focuses on highlighting the weakness with which contemporary thought believes it can eliminate the traditional concept of truth. In fact, the decline of traditional thought was simply inevitable because it was nothing more than the becoming self-coherent of the basic error of all Western philosophy: the belief that beings can oscillate between being and nothingness. This becoming self-coherent consists of positing irrevocably that if something oscillates between being and nothing, then everything can oscillate, and no God (or immutable) is necessary to justify the becoming of the world. If philosophical thought, in its initial configuration, has thought of the immutable as the condition of possibility of the existence of the becoming of the world, in its most coherent development it has come to the conclusion that if becoming exists (that is, if things oscillate between being and non-being), then no immutable being can exist. The goal of *Law and Chance* is to identify the dynamics that produce the decline of traditional thought and of its willingness to define truth in an unconfutable way. The existence of every 'immutable being' negates becoming, and this is the reason for the rejection of traditional thought, which would have wanted to reduce the contingent world (as that which can indifferently occur or not occur) to such absolute norms. Contemporary criticism is based on the awareness that every eternal (absolute) being should want to impose itself on the totality of beings and therefore demand that everything be subjected to it. Severino emphasises that the basis of every theoretical disinterest is a practical interest: 'Pure seeing [which traditional philosophy has understood as disinterested knowledge] is praxis: in fact, the most powerful form of praxis that can exist in the history of the West before the appearance of modern science' (*Law and Chance*). The incontrovertible truth evoked by the Greeks is in fact a form of absolute power on becoming, and the prediction of every possible happening: it is a prediction because there is nothing of the present, of the past and of the future that can escape to its legislation; but just because it reaches the present, the most distant past and the most distant future, it constitutes an infallible prediction and an absolute power on the becoming of the world. As absolute dominion over becoming, the *epistéme* (as Greek thought calls the stable knowledge that cannot be disproved) annihilates not only any attempt to go beyond the limit imposed by any supreme legislation, but also the very becoming of the world. It is this essential feature of the *epistéme* (its being a dominant and annihilating knowledge) that marks the passage from epistemic predictions to scientific ones, and to the experimental method. The epistemic legislation also reaches what, not having happened yet, is still nothing, anticipating its essential meaning by transforming what is still nothing into an already existing thing – thus cancelling all the unpredictability of becoming. In this way, the coming out from nothing is reduced to a mere appearance. But for the same *epistéme* and for the West, becoming is what is not erasable, because the becoming of things is the *maximum evident*. Since the submission to an eternal being would cancel the contingent character of all events – that is, the possibility of understanding them as being nothing before they happen and after they have happened – any absolute (immutable) is critically rejected by the profound essence of contemporary philosophy and epistemology: the decisive argument that swirls beneath the surface of the thought of our time is the faith in the becoming of things, a faith that is destined to sweep away any absolute truth that differs from that of which that faith is the full expression. Then, science and technique can explain everything without any hypostatization of absolute beings. This is the cornerstone of *Law and Chance*.

The fifth axis, which entirely involves the scientific observation of phenomena, is inherent in the way we observe any facts and interpret them. *Law and Chance* also includes the 'Introduction' to Severino's translation[3] of Carnap's *Der Logische Aufbau der Welt* and the discussion of Carnap's philosophy. The strict analysis of the logic-positivistic position inherent to what appears is also a significant task, which Severino undertakes precisely in order to analyse one of the most coherent manifestations of contemporary philosophy's subordination to science. This analysis, however, shows how the concept of 'appearing' in Severino's thought is radical but also so cogent that it could also be assumed by even the most rigorous neo-positivist thinkers. Actually, the rigorous observation of what appears permits us to say that it is impossible to say that we can observe an act of creation and an act of annihilation. It is absolutely impossible to say that 'nothingness' appears. Severino shows that, contrary to what Western philosophy assumes, no becoming appears in the sense of the appearing of the annihilation or of the becoming *ex nihilo* of beings. It is thus incorrect to say that Severino's perspective denies experience, and that claiming the eternity of every being amounts to denying the manifold display of what appears. On the contrary,

Severino contends that the content that actually appears does not testify to the annihilation and creation of beings in any way. Appearing and experience cannot attest to what no longer belongs or to what does not yet belong to experience, has become nothing or is still nothing. To consider the 'becoming' testified by experience as a coming from or returning to nothingness is thus only the content of a 'faith'. The different forms in which this faith in the fundamental error is manifested compete with each other. Throughout history, the winning manifestation of the different expressions of faith has unfolded. Today, the dominant faith in the evidence of becoming demands that the only possible science is scientific theory understood as hypothetical anticipation of events. *Law and Chance* discusses this specific form of scientific faith and its power. What clearly emerges is the essential meaning of the 'destruction' of the immutables of the epistemic tradition by contemporary thought. The 'event' comes from its own nothingness, and therefore it is 'chance': it is becoming understood as the sphere in which things come out of nothingness and return to nothingness. It is exactly this (Greek) understanding of the becoming that is at the basis of modern science and constitution of the same experimental method. In fact, if in the process of experience things come out from nothing and they return to nothing, such a process cannot be anticipated if not in a hypothetical form. And the experimental method assumes that any scientific theory or model may be changeable because of the unpredictability of chance. Well, if in the process of experience things come out from nothing and they return to nothing, such a process cannot be anticipated if not in a hypothetical form. The

Greek sense of becoming necessarily brings to an end every metaphysical-philosophical conception of theory and imposes as the only possible form of 'theory' the one that is constituted not as an incontrovertible rule of the event, but as an open hypothesis: 'In this respect, every scientific law (be that causal or probabilistic) is a law of chance' (*Law and Chance*). What escapes the self-consciousness of scientific knowledge, remaining trapped in the unconscious of the process in which modern science itself consists, is the Greek soul of its own essence: 'Contemporary culture has, by now, acquired a thorough awareness of the hypothetical character of science, as well as of its extreme possibilities of domination. What, instead, keeps being overlooked is that modern science is the most powerful form of domination because it is the one that best conforms to the Greek meaning of becoming' (*Law and Chance*). By ignoring this hidden essence, scientific knowledge cannot prevent the epistemic attitude that introduces immutable forms (e.g. determinism in the theory of relativity) from reappearing in it (in the most diverse forms), which are nevertheless objectively overcome. But in its deepest essence, the philosophy of our time shows the inevitability of the death of absolute metaphysical-epistemic truth: it brings to coherence the fundamental principle of Western thought, namely the persuasion that the becoming of the world is the supreme self-evidence, thereby peremptorily denying that there can be an eternal reality that regulates this oscillation. (Thinkers such as Giacomo Leopardi, Friedrich Nietzsche and Giovanni Gentile, to whom Severino has dedicated important studies, would come to this mature awareness.) The extreme fidelity to the (presumed) original self-evidence of the 'event' (i.e., of becoming) brings to an end every metaphysical-epistemic conception of theory, and opens the space in which techno-science can exercise its dominion over things.

Law and Chance, however, should be collocated in the entire path of Severino's discourse, which, while pointing at the extreme error, also shows its recognisability through its relation with the 'non-error' – that is, what he calls the 'originary structure' (*struttura originaria*) and later the 'originary structure of the destiny of truth'[4]: the undeniable appearing of every being's self-being as that whose negation is self-negation. To deny that being is not non-being (i.e for the opposition of the positive and the negative to be *effectively* denied), it is necessary for the difference between being and non-being to appear as affirmed, otherwise we would not be dealing with a denial of the identity/ non-contradiction of being:

> In order to have a real negation of the opposition (and not merely an apparent one), it is necessary that the positive and the negative should first be posited as different (and so as opposites), and that one then posit the identity of the differents, i.e., that the differents *qua* differents are identical. As long as the differents are not seen as different, they must unquestionably be said to be identical; but if they are seen as different, and if, indeed, they must be held fast as different, in order that the affirmation of their identity may be negation of the opposition of the positive and the negative, then this negation is grounded upon the affirmation of what it denies.[5]

It follows that the denial of the difference (of the positive and the negative) by denying its own foundation, denies itself. Nihilism, as the alienation of authentic truth, is self-negating, and thus, starting from the destiny of truth, both epistemic metaphysics and contemporary thought are forms of the alienation of truth. The impossibility of the existence of a time in which beings that appear are 'not yet' or 'no longer' founds the impossibility of any creation and annihilation. And 'it is impossible' means that the claim that 'a being is not' is the negation of the originary structure, and more specifically, it is the negation of the opposition of the positive and the negative; it is the claim that being is other than itself. This means that they negate the fundamental principles of any logical assertion: the principle of identity, the principle of non-contradiction and the principle of the third excluded. This implicit negation is the basis of the self-negation that the *élenchos* makes explicit.

Severino reaches this conclusion after identifying the most ancient origin of the process, which started with the 'path of night', that consists in the extreme alienation of thought, which has always been opposed by a different path, the 'path of day'. Western philosophy achieves full coherence by denying the traditional way of defining truth, but in this way, it expresses its most profound alienation. In *Law and Chance*, Severino illustrates the reasons why the strongest power today is technology, guided by modern science, and why the planet is destined to the civilization of technology (which, however, is in turn destined to a time in which this technological paradise will decline). In *Law and Chance*, Severino analyses, in particular, neo-positivism in its transition from its semantic phase (early Wittgenstein, Schlick, early Carnap) – where the validity of scientific language was placed in its reference to 'facts', and where propositions expressing the immediate contents of experience are posited as indubitable truth – to the syntactic approach (Neurath, the second Carnap, Popper), in which the objectivity of scientific language is not understood as the absolute truth of the propositions of science, but as their intersubjectivity, in the conviction that authentic knowledge can be nothing other than intersubjective knowledge. In fact, it is the coherent development of the will to power that destroys everything that would nullify that becoming of the world that, for Western civilisation, is instead valid as the original self-evidence. What the critical self-consciousness of science fails to perceive, however, is that the same 'inclusion of the datum in the context of an intersubjective consensus, or lack thereof – the inclusion with which the datum obtains a scientific value – is an interpretation' (*Law and Chance*). And it is precisely on the theme of the intersubjectivity of scientific knowledge that, in *Law and Chance*, Severino examines the last great project for a unitary arrangement of culture: Carnap's system of constitution – in which the unifying and subordinating principle is no longer a philosophical-metaphysical-theological horizon, but a scientific one, and where it is precisely the instance of intersubjectivity 'comes in this way to be fully accountable for the rejection of metaphysics' (*Law and Chance*). The history of the West is the history of the will to power that frees itself of everything that would frustrate its effective exercise. Thus, linguistic mediation presents itself as the concrete place of becoming within which things are continually produced and transformed. For Severino, this is the history of the essential alienation of a thought that, in wanting things to become something else, wants, in its unconscious, things to be nothing – wants the impossible.

Finally, it is important to revisit the final specific feature of Severino's indication, which lies beyond the present clash between tradition and the civilisation of techno-science, both driven by the same persuasion that things oscillate between being and non-being. Please note: the content indicated by Emanuele Severino's writings is certainly the negation of the error and the erring in which that persuasion consists, but it does not annul the error – which in itself is nothing – nor does it annul the erring, but sees the nullity of the content of the erring and the essential self-supersession of the erring. (In this sense, it is not even correct to say that Severino's discourse is anti-traditional, and anti-contemporary. It is not correct to the extent that the prefix 'anti' indicates some will to annul what is denied). If the coming from and the return to nothingness cannot appear, this means that the variations in the world are the appearing and disappearing of beings, and this appears incontrovertibly. Thus, it must be the case that every variation in the world is the beginning of the appearing of the eternal beings that did not appear before, or the no-longer-appearing of the eternal beings that appeared before; beginning and ceasing to appear do not mean beginning and ceasing to be, but entering and leaving the horizon of appearing.

The Translation of Destiny, and the Destiny of Translation

DAMIANO SACCO

The theoretical elements required in order to understand the meaning of translation in Emanuele Severino's thought – namely, according to 'the language that testifies to destiny' [*il linguaggio che testimonia il destino*] – have not, as of yet, appeared in English; that is to say, they have not yet been translated. The very question of translation can, however, serve as a key guiding axis for introducing some of the most fundamental elements of Severino's testimony. This testimony bears in fact witness to the appearing of a content that cannot be translated, and testifies precisely to the appearing of this untranslatability. Testimony, appearing, translation: the following remarks aim to delineate the extent to which these three dimensions articulate the same matter according to three indissociable axes.

The tradition of the West – but, as it will be argued, every tradition *qua* tradition – is in its essence the history of the figures of translation: the translation between the One and the many, matter and form, potentiality and actuality, being and appearing, spirit and nature. The tradition of translation unfolds according to the primary determinations of what comes to be regarded, in that very tradition, as the history of philosophy: *mímesis, méthexis, kínesis, aporrhoé, adaequatio*, relationship between primary and secondary qualities, between appearance and thing in itself, between being-in-itself and being-for-us, between being and appearing. Translation results in the appearing of what appears; what comes to be referred to as the history of Western metaphysics coincides with the history of the indissoluble link between being, appearing and translation: the 'end' of the history of metaphysics marks the breaking down of the paradigm that governs the structure of this link. Accordingly, the framework of translation is no longer able to express the truth of being and appearing.

The last century has extensively testified to the breaking down of this paradigm, and has witnessed the appearing of different 'readings' and interpretations of the tradition of the West (one may think, for instance, of the different destructions [*Destruktion, Abbau*] and deconstructions of the history of Western metaphysics); and yet, precisely insofar as these hermeneutical attempts have been advanced *qua* readings and interpretations – namely, insofar as they have *not* emerged from an element of necessity – they have (this time *of necessity*) overlooked that the interpretative (or, one could say, translational) character constitutes, in fact, the very essence of tradition. These critical readings have thus come to partake in the essence of the very tradition that they set out to critically interpret.

Emanuele Severino's testimony stands out precisely in this respect: for it is only by recognising that translation constitutes not only the essence of the interpretations of the tradition of the West, but the essence of this very tradition, that the necessity of the way in which any tradition understands itself, and its interpretations, may begin to emerge.

According to a set of well-known etymological considerations, every tradition constitutes a form of betrayal: 'tradition' (*traditio*) and 'be-trayal' (from Old French *traïr*) both originate from the Latin *tradere* (this is even clearer in the Italian terms *tradizione* [tradition] and *tradire* [betray]). That is to say, what is handed over (*tradere*: *trans-dare*) to posterity is with one and the same gesture betrayed (*traditus*) – Christ is be-trayed (*traditus*) by Judas precisely insofar as he is handed over (*trans-datus*). Etymology, however, does not at first appear to be able to account for the shared essence of tradition and translation (*trans-latus* originates from *trans-fero*, *not* from *tradere*; similarly for the Italian *traduco*, from *trans-duco*): namely, for the claim that the betrayal of every tradition consists in a certain translation. The essential betrayal at the core of every translation, history and tradition, however, has nothing to do with any generic notion of inaccuracy or inexactness within what comes to be handed over, translated or entrusted within a tradition: the 'betrayal' at stake is instead a betrayal of the essence of what is and appears, a betrayal that lies with the *trans-* that is present (this time also etymologically) in every tradition and translation (*trans-do, trans-fero, trans-duco*).

It is precisely the betrayal of translation, the betrayal of any trans-ferral, becoming or motion – which is, throughout the tradition of the West, understood primarily according to its *translational* mode (*phorá, kínesis katà tópon*) – that Severino identifies as the mark of every tradition (and, in particular, of the tradition of the West). And yet, according to Severino, this very betrayal is impossible – it is *the* impossible: nothing, nothingness itself. There can be no translation, no betrayal, no tradition. Nothing that is and appears can be other than what it is, other than itself – *translatus, traditus*. Within Severino's testimony, the error of translation constitutes the 'folly' of every tradition: the betrayal of the truth of being, the translation of the untranslatable.

Every testimony, however, differs from the content it testifies to; every testimony constitutes a translation – and, therefore, a betrayal – of the content that it testifies to: every witness differs from what it bears witness to. But if no translation is possible (and, therefore, no testimony, for any testimony represents a translation) how can the language that testifies to destiny – testify? How can Severino's testimony appear, and how can it differ from other impossible testimonies? And, lastly, how can the language that testifies to destiny – a language that testifies that any translation is incontrovertibly impossible, nothing – be itself translated?

The translation of destiny

In order to answer these guiding questions, it is necessary to recall some of the fundamental elements of the language that testifies to the destiny of necessity. As Severino would repeatedly remark, the answers provided here necessarily lack the element of necessity that pertains to them, a necessity that could only originate from showing how these determinations originate from the concrete structure of meaning that represents the concrete meaning of necessity itself: the originary structure of the truth of being – that whose negation negates itself, the incontrovertible truth of being. *The Essence of Nihilism* (London: Verso, 2016) already shows that the originary structure – the self-being of being, every being's self-being – necessarily entails the eternity of all beings. This gesture, this thought, this fear, their appearing – every being that is and appears – is and cannot not be; as such, every being is eternal. The spectacle of becoming does not consist of an impossible transition – an impossible translation – between being and nothingness; according to Severino, the originary structure entails that becoming can only consist of the appearing and disappearing of the eternal beings – a process in which no translation takes place: one after the other, the eternal beings enter and leave the circle of appearing, but through this process they are eternally saved from any annihilation. Not even their appearing can turn into nothingness: the appearing of every being (which is itself a being that is and appears) is itself saved in the eternity of being, as it enters and leaves the circle of appearing (according to a determinate structure that cannot be presented here; the reader should refer to 'Returning to Parmenides' and its 'Postscript' collected in *The Essence of Nihilism*).

The first element that pertains to the present discussion emerges here. According to Severino, the originary structure of the truth of being entails that there can be no translation between being and appearing, between a being that is and *the same* being as it appears. Any 'translation', any difference, between a being *qua* it appears and a being *qua* it does not yet appear or it no longer does so – namely, any translation or transition attributed to the appearing of becoming – would necessarily constitute the annihilation of some determinations: precisely, of those determinations that are translated, and that therefore *are*, as long as the being appears, and *are not* when the being no longer appears. The translation between being and appearing – the becoming or appearing of beings – entails the existence of a time in which a determination-that-is is not: the impossible.

Every being is, on the contrary, the *immediate* self-identity of a meaning that cannot be transformed: a meaning that cannot be translated, and which as such is saved in the eternity of being. The tradition of the West – but, once again, *every* tradition that constitutes a form of be-trayal of the truth of being – consists of a faith in the taking place of an impossible translation between being and nothingness: the translation that constitutes the becoming and appearing of beings. Severino testifies to this impossibility: the impossibility of transforming or translating any text, any language, any being. Every 'text' is untranslatable, and, thus, eternal.

The possibility (and necessity) of translation

Severino's testimony – the language that testifies to destiny – constitutes, precisely, *a testimony*: namely, an account, given in the form of a human language, which appears for the most part through the writings of a certain empirical person, and which is connected to the totality of determinations that constitute its singular appearance. This testimony, like every other testimony, appears to differ from what it testifies to – except that, in this instance, what is testified to is precisely what *cannot* differ. What is testified to is what cannot be other than itself, the originary meaning of being: being's self-being, being's impossibility of not coinciding with itself and with its own being. For if any being were to be other than itself, it would not be: a being (something that is) would be nothingness. Every testimony, insofar as it is and appears, constitutes a testimony to the truth of being; but the 'difference' between the truth of being and the content of any human testimony is in fact infinitely more abyssal than what can be testified to by any human testimony.

Every human sign, insofar as it is supposed to designate a meaning, is abstracted from the totality in which it appears – precisely in order to constitute an idealised and reproducible sign. It is this abstraction – this extraction or isolation of a part from the totality of being – that constitutes the essential translation that throughout the tradition of the West betrays the truth of being: for both the sign and the designated meaning, *qua* abstracted, differ from themselves *qua* belonging to the totality in which they appear. But precisely insofar as they differ from what is – and given that everything that is cannot be other than itself – they are not: they are nothing. Everything – every thing, being, sign, gesture, will – cannot but fail to indicate the meaning it attempts to indicate: it cannot but fail to do so because it must first of all fail to be an 'abstract' or 'separated' sign (a sign isolated from the totality in which it appears, a sign which would therefore be different from itself as contained in that totality). Concurrently, every meaning designated by a sign must itself fail to be separated from the totality of being (for otherwise, once again, what is would be other than itself: something-that-is would be nothing, which is the originary meaning of impossibility).

This is the essential translation that constitutes every tradition: namely, the translation that believes to be able to abstract and isolate a part of the concrete totality of being – a translation that, were it to be successful, would result in the impossible identification of being and nothingness. This is the essential translation or alienation that according to Severino constitutes the history of nihilism – what Severino names the history of the 'folly' – the 'isolated earth': the 'earth' (the appearing content) that is separated or 'isolated' from the concrete totality of the truth of being. The 'isolated earth' constitutes the failed attempt at translating the concrete totality of being; every translation, according to Severino's testimony, would constitute a translation of being into nothingness. As a result, every translation is incontrovertibly impossible.

And, indeed, the translations of the history of nihilism do not appear: for nothingness is not and cannot appear (no translation that would abstract a part of the concrete totality of being can appear). Every testimony, including the language that testifies to the destiny of necessity, constitutes on the contrary a belief, or faith, in the existence of these abstractions: namely, a will that wills the existence of these translations. Every translation consists, as such, of a will that wills that something be other than itself. Since no being, however, can be other than what it itself is, every translation consists of a will that wills nothingness itself. While this nothingness is not and cannot appear, these beliefs, faiths and wills have, within the concrete totality of being, a completely different meaning – namely a completely different self-identity – as parts of the untranslatable totality (these parts, Severino would insist, are 'distinguished' rather than 'separated' within this totality). It is within this totality that the contradictions of translation appear as negated by the originary untranslatable meaning of being.

A testimony of untranslatability

Having outlined the structure of the appearing of empirical testimonies, the next question concerns the status of Severino's own testimony. That is to say, granting that all human testimonies constitute a failed attesmpt at abstracting signs and meanings, signifiers and signifieds, why should one pay any special regard to this particular testimony (which, in spite of its unheard-of content, still remains a human testimony)? Once again, if all human languages constitute a will that attempts to translate the concrete meaning of being (namely, the failed attempt at abstracting or transforming the totality of being), why should Severino's testimony be any different? The discussion becomes here rapidly technical.

Severino is in this respect unambiguous: the language that testifies to destiny cannot but be a human language – a will that wills that certain signs should indicate certain other meanings. The language that testifies to destiny is itself part of the 'isolated earth', and constitutes an impossible translation. And yet, *within* the alienated or abstract domain, there is 'one' language that sets itself apart from all other ones: for while all testimonies that belong to the history of nihilism speak with alienated words, the language that testifies to destiny is the only testimony that speaks – albeit still in alienated terms – of *its own alienation*, of its own being an impossible translation. Severino writes:

> The alteration of destiny accomplished by the language that testifies to it differs from the alteration that asserts the becoming-other of beings. This latter assertion not only *is* (like that language) a will to make things become other, but it also *affirms* their becoming-other, and hence *affirms* what it itself *is*. On the other hand, the testimony of destiny *is* indeed a will to make destiny, *qua* being, become other, but it *negates* the becoming-other of beings, and hence *negates* what it itself is.
>
> *La morte e la terra*, Milan: Adelphi, 2011, p. 128

The present translation is, as well, certainly part of the history of alienation: it is the result of a will ('mine'), which believes it is able to transform and modify a certain text; it consists in the belief that this text constitutes a translation of a certain other text. And yet, this translation testifies *in its content* to the impossibility of translation *per se*: it testifies to the impossibility of what it, necessarily, believes to be. In other words – but here the technical dimension truly exceeds the present discussion – the language that testifies to destiny shares with the concrete totality of being 'a segment of identity' that *differs* from the segment of identity shared by all other alienated testimonies (where every abstract part, *qua* 'distinguished' rather than 'separated' within the concrete totality, shares with that totality a 'segment of identity').

Translating a testimony of untranslatability

Having outlined the way in which the appearing of the language that testifies to destiny differs from the appearing of other testimonies, there remains the question of how to understand the present translation. Namely, what does it mean to translate a testimony that asserts the very alienated and impossible nature of translation itself? We should recall here that, according to what has been said so far, the appearing of 'the original' language that testifies to destiny ('Severino's'), as well as of its translation, consists of the appearing of the eternal beings that one after the other enter and leave 'the circle of appearing' – the stage of the spectacle of appearing – without in so doing handing over anything to nothingness (not even their very appearing, which is itself an eternal being that enters and leaves unscathed the circle of appearing). That a certain text is the 'translation' of another one ('the original') means that, within the concrete totality of being, a certain meaning (a certain set of eternal beings) is shared by the two sets of beings that constitute the 'original' and the 'translation' (it should be noted that this shared meaning is a reciprocal relation that invalidates the identification of one of the two texts with 'the original' and the other one with 'the translation'). If two 'texts' are related to one another according to this generalised notion of translation, then the sets of eternals that constitute these two texts must share, in the concrete totality of being, a certain segment of identity, for otherwise the two texts would not appear to be connected by a relationship of translation (granting that every being must partake of the meaning of being). The concrete determinations of this shared meaning can vary considerably, thus giving rise to different notions of translation and adaptation of a text (one may think of the meanings shared by a text and its translations into different languages, by different versions of the 'same' myth, by a text and its screen or stage adaptations, and so forth). The appearing of this shared meaning, which is *indifferent* to the very differences that accompany it within different languages and adaptations, will be explored in the next of Severino's texts to be translated into English, *Oltre il linguaggio* [*Beyond Language*] (Milan: Adelphi, 1992).

Let us nevertheless remark that the translations of the language that testifies to destiny stand out among all empirical translations in the same way in which the testimony of the destiny of necessity differs from other empirical testimonies. For, in addition to the identical (complex) meaning that is shared by a text and its translation, a second singular meaning is shared by the language that testifies to destiny and its translation: namely, the meaning that negates the very possibility of translation as understood throughout the history of translation and nihilism – a meaning that belongs both to the 'original' testimony of destiny and to its translations (if they are such). That is to say, this translation still consists of a will to modify and transform a certain text (and, therefore, it still consists of the belief that this will has obtained what it willed), but it testifies, at the same time, to the very impossibility of any such will or translation.

The destiny of translation

Every translation consists of a will that attempts to transform a certain 'text'. According to this will (namely, according to every tradition that, *qua* tradition, translates and transforms), every thing and every being are part of a (generalised) text – they are part of a system of abstract signs that a will believes to be able to transform, create and destroy. According to Severino's testimony, the will to transform a certain text, or parts of it, constitutes the impossible: the originary meaning of impossibility. As such, the essence of translation constitutes the essence of our tradition: the essence of nihilism – the essence of technics. According to Severino, we recall here, the essence of technics is the essence of every production or *poíesis*: the impossible production of being out of nothingness ('Everything that is responsible for creating being out of nothingness is a kind of *poíesis*', *Symposium* 205b–c, cf. *Sophist* 219b, 265b; 'the productions of every *téchne* are a kind of *poíesis*', *Symposium* 205c).

The destiny of translation is, accordingly, indissociable from the destiny of technics. And not only insofar as technology will of necessity take over the task of the translator – for, indeed, the essence of translation always coincides with the essence of technics, even when empirical translations are not completely entrusted to technology – but in the extremely more radical sense that the essence of translation coincides with the essence of technics, of nihilism and of tradition: with the will that wills nothingness itself. The essence shared by the destiny of translation and by the destiny of technics entails, according to a necessity testified to by Severino, that all those structures of texts and languages that still oppose any resistance to the will that wills the complete transformability of every being should come to be destroyed (including any persistence of signs, meanings, texts, languages). The destiny of translation entails that every (generalised) text – and, therefore, every (generalised) language – should come of necessity to appear in their pure oscillation (*epamphoterízein*) between being and nothingness: that is to say, in their pure translatability.

Severino – the language that bears witness to the destiny of necessity – testifies to the destiny of technics, and, thus, to the destiny of translation. The most crucial step forward taken by this language consists in a testimony of the necessity with which the twilight of the history of nihilism is to occur: the twilight of the history of technics and translation (*La Gloria*, Milan: Adelphi, 2001). The twilight of the history of translation marks the twilight of the will that believes it is able to abstract and transform meanings, beings, texts, and languages; it marks the appearing of the concrete self-identity of every appearing content: the end of the translations that believe to abstract the untranslatable concreteness of being into nothingness. According to Severino, however, the coming to pass of this twilight (the coming to pass of the 'saving earth') entails the necessary appearing of the concrete totality of the alienated or translated earth (the 'Good Friday' of the isolation of the earth). The coming to pass of this twilight is also anticipated by the epoch in which the peoples of the earth speak the language that testifies to destiny (*Oltrepassare*, Milan: Adelphi, 2007; *Storia, Gioia*, Milan: Adelphi, 2016). However, it does not yet concretely appear how the translations of the language that testifies to destiny in other languages may lead to the coming to pass of that epoch, and, thus, to the culmination of the destiny of translation.

Law and chance

The principal note to the present translation concerns the term 'chance' (*caso*). The semantic connection – and, even more, the philosophical one – between 'chance' and the 'falling' and 'befalling' of events might not immediately be apparent. While the English language preserves the explicit connection between what falls and what be-falls, it draws these two terms from proto-Germanic, while drawing the word 'chance' from Old French, and, ultimately, from Latin (*cadere*). Italian, on the other hand, draws all three terms from Latin: *caso* (chance), *cadere* (fall) and *accadere* (befall). Despite the different etymological origins, both languages preserve the semantic connection between the three words: what be-falls [*ac-cade*] is, precisely, what falls [*cade*] into existence – chance constitutes precisely this falling into existence, 'a be-falling that falls out of nothingness [*un accadere che cade da niente*]'. It is from this semantic connection – a connection that in Italian is also reflected in the etymology – that Severino draws his philosophical argument.

According to Severino, chance – insofar as it is 'an emerging from nothingness, a falling upon existence without having been thrown by anything' – constitutes the very essence of the thing (of every thing) *qua* this has been thought by the West: namely, the thing insofar as it becomes ('becoming', Severino writes 'is the be-falling [*ac-cadere*] of events that issue from their own nothingness'). Everything that befalls falls into existence emerging out of nothing: everything happens by chance. That, in modern physics, every law should come to take a probabilistic form is then nothing short of a necessity that follows from the very essence of chance as thought according to the Greek meanings of being and nothingness.

The very essence of being as thought by the West lies, according to Severino, with this fall, and with the notion of a most temporary and provisional balance of being on the presence of the present time. Being is (in) time precisely to the extent that it is always liable to fall off the present into the nothingness of the future and of the past. Severino writes in *Destino della necessità*:

> Time is the *ptôsis* of being (*ptôsis rématos*; *De Interpretatione*, 16b, 17): the 'fall' of being outside the 'is' into the 'will be' and the 'was' (into the 'still nothing' and the 'no longer anything') – being's balancing itself on the 'is' of the temporal present, while always being liable to fall upon the past or the future. Being is *ptôsis* – that is, time – precisely because things are a form of *epamphoterízein* between being and nothingness.
>
> *Destino della necessità*, Milan: Adelphi, 1980, p. 154

The 'destiny of necessity' constitutes, on the contrary, precisely the site where being – every being – is forever saved from an impossible fall into nothingness.

Lastly, a very brief note on the translation of the term '*originario*'. This word, which is perhaps *the* Severinian word par excellence, cannot immediately be translated without any residues into any ordinary English word, and has furthermore acquired a singular and hardly translatable meaning through the (vast) set of Severino's writings. It is for this reason that it has been translated by the – perhaps slightly idiosyncratic – English word 'originary', in the hope that this may in turn become one of the words most immediately connected to Severino's philosophical corpus. The word '*originario*' is in fact considerably more customary in the Italian language than 'originary' is in English (it should be noted, however, that 'originary' is not as of yet marked by dictionaries as being 'obsolete'), but many ordinary

English words (e.g. original, primary, primal) carry additional semantic components that are alien to the Italian meaning (original may additionally be attributed to something innovative or creative, primary to something which is first among others, primal to something that is primordial or primeval). Furthermore, a most extensive semantic volume has accrued upon this word through virtually all of the thousands of pages that Severino has written (and yet, this meaning has also remained, *at the same time*, within the unchangeable confines delineated for the first time by *La struttura originaria*; Milan: Adelphi, 1981). It thus appears that the word 'originary' might both come closest to the meaning of '*originario*' and, precisely by virtue of its being out of immediate customary use, provide a neutral ground for the sedimentation of an unheard-of semantic volume. (It should be noted that a similar problem has occurred with the translation of the word '*ursprünglich*' in many of Martin Heidegger's writings, a problem which has also often been solved by means of the word 'originary'.)

Note on the Text

The essay in Part I of this volume is the inaugural lecture delivered at the conference '*Induzione, probabilità, statistica*' ['Induction, Probability, Statistics'] held at the University of Venice in September of 1978. The essay in Part II revisits, with an eye to the questions unfolded in the first essay, the Introduction to the Italian edition of *Der logische Aufbau der Welt – Scheinprobleme in der Philosophie* by Rudolf Carnap (*La costruzione logica del mondo*, trans. and Introduction by E. Severino, Turin: Utet, 1997).

Part One

Law and chance

The Immutables, Nothingness, Chance

I

In certain sectors of contemporary culture, there is still a widespread conviction as to the idea that, once the homogeneity and convergence of science and domination are established, the negative and alienating character of science will, by the same token, appear as self-evident. But it is precisely in relation to the meaning of the negative and of alienation that the difficulties become insurmountable. Why should domination not be exerted? And exerted without limits? Perhaps because it results in the violation of human rights? But which knowledge is able, at this point, to exhibit the *true* rights [*diritti*] and to establish the *true* limit that separates the law [*il diritto*] from the crookedness of humans?

In the history of the West, the knowledge that has taken it upon itself to exhibit *truth* is philosophy: that is, 'science' –

regarded not in the modern sense, but as *epistéme*. According to what the Greek word itself suggests, this is the knowledge whose content is able *to stand*, firmly imposing itself *on* everything that would like to displace it and put it into question. This is the knowledge that, precisely by virtue of its standing, is truth.

By now, however, philosophy has died; the dream of a definitive and incontrovertible truth is over: not only for the forces that promote the development of the civilisation of technics [*civiltà della tecnica*], but also for all those forms of humanism that, while being nurtured by the death of philosophy, are nevertheless deluded about being able to counter this violence – perpetrated by technics and scientific knowledge – by laying claim to human rights. If the dream of truth is over, then the word 'truth' cannot but signify a capacity for domination – that is, power [*potenza*] – and the word 'error' cannot but signify a form of impotence [*impotenza*]. The 'truth' of a theory is decided by a practical conflict with the opponent; this is also the meaning of Marx's second thesis on Feuerbach. Which also means, however, that class exploitation and the violation of human rights are not symptoms of an 'injustice' – for the death of the truth of the *epistéme* is also the death of what justice truly is – but are symptoms of an impotence: that is, symptoms of the 'error' to which the exploited classes and those who are subjected to violence belong.

Modern science, *qua* theoretical and technical structure, is the highest form of power, and therefore of 'truth', that exists today on earth. The forces of religion, faith, morals, the unconscious, affect, ideological and political thought are by now powerless against the force of science. This means neither that science constitutes itself independently from society nor that the social organisation is not still determined by religious, moral, ideological and affective forces. It rather means that the organisation of society, and therefore of science itself, is today all the more efficient – all the more powerful – the more the criteria that regulate the social organisation come to coincide with the criteria of scientific rationality, and therefore the more the *ideological* organisation and administration of science become the *scientific* organisation and administration of science.

II

Modern science is the most powerful form of domination because it is the most powerful form of prediction. A prediction [*previsione*] anticipates a vision [*visione*] that does not yet exist: either because the object of the vision does not yet exist or because the conditions that let the object become visible do not do so. A prediction is established not only in relation to the current non-existence of a vision, but also in relation to the vision that, within the prediction, is conceived of as something that sooner or later will begin to exist. Predictions constitute themselves within *an experience of the becoming of the world* – that is, within the process in which the objects of the vision (or the conditions that make them visible) begin to exist. A vision is, then, what the scientific language calls a 'verification' or 'falsification' of a prediction.

Domination, however, is precisely domination of the becoming of the world. Precisely because becoming is a coming into existence, it is the irruption of the unforeseen and of the unprecedented: that which, by virtue of its radical novelty and unpredictability, threatens every existing thing – threatens the existence of every thing. The will to be saved from the threat of becoming is one of the originary forms of domination. Every form of salvation (such as, for instance, the Christian one) belongs to the will to salvation that coincides with domination. In order to be saved, it is necessary to contain the threat of becoming: namely, it is necessary to control it, to subject it to a law, and therefore to dominate it. Vice-versa, in order to dominate, it is first of all necessary not to be swept away by the irruption of the unpredictable, and thereby be saved from it.

But since the threat is given, precisely, by the absolute unpredictability of the becoming of the world, it is necessary to somehow make the unpredictable predictable in order to contain [*arginare*] the threat. The banks [*l'argine*] are able to hold only if the forces that press against them are not absolutely unpredictable and unknown. The originary bank is, in fact, the prediction itself: namely, the will to anticipate (*ante-capere*) and pre-capture the events that arise. Indeed, predictions entail that becoming should no longer be a terrifying vision of the irruption of the absolutely unforeseen, but rather the vision of a process that conforms to what has been predicted. For this reason, becoming is a conformity to an order, or to a law, which does not let itself be swept away by the irruption of events, but rather controls, dominates and grounds the abyss of becoming.

III

Asserting that science is the most powerful form of domination because it is the most powerful form of prediction entails that science stands at the end of the history of domination.

Already in the prehistory of domination, among the populations that come before the history of the West, predictions dominate the irruption of becoming by anticipating an immutable order within the succession of events. This anticipation finds its fundamental expression in the archaic myth of the eternal return. The archetypal determinations of the cosmogenic circle are the immutable order to which every becoming must conform.

But it is only with the beginning of Western civilisation, with Greek thought, that the meaning indicated by the words 'succession', 'becoming', 'return', 'event', 'immutable order' and 'eternal' comes explicitly to the forefront. The whole of Western civilisation unfolds according to the Greek meaning of these words. And it is precisely with Greek thought that, with an unprecedented rigour and lucidity, predictions begin to dominate becoming through the invocation of the immutable and eternal beings: that is, of those structures that are not swept away by the becoming of the world, but contain its threat, and close ranks around what, at every turn, the inhabitants of the West regard as being inalienable. Predicting means willing that becoming (time, history) should conform to the order that has been predicted; but this order must be an immutable one if the threat of becoming is not to constitute itself, once again, as a real possibility.

To this end, not only is it necessary that the predicted order should be an immutable one, but also that it should be impossible for a prediction to fail and turn into a different prediction. Accordingly, predictions must be incontrovertible, and must firmly stand by themselves. To the extent that they *stand*, predictions overcome the instability of myths and become, precisely, *epistéme*: namely, knowledge that firmly *stands* in opposition (*epí*) to all conflicting opinions. The immutable and eternal beings predicted by predictions are not an illusion only if predictions themselves are *epistéme*. The preposition *epí*, however, does not only refer to the conflicting opinions *over* (*epí*) which the *epistéme* dominates, but it also refers to all the events that can arise – *over* which, once again, predictions dominate. The *epistéme* dominates over *all* events; it is a gaze that anticipates *the whole*: everything that already exists, and everything that can exist and does not yet exist. The threat of becoming is defeated, rather than simply being deferred, only if an epistemic prediction casts its gaze at the whole and not simply at a part – the configuration of which could suddenly be swept away by the irruption of the unforeseen.

The birth of philosophy consists – according to the Platonic-Aristotelian account – in the positing of the 'principle' of all the things that are born and perish. This is the positing of an immutable unity that gathers together all becoming things, both those that are alike and close-by as well as those that are different and far apart: this 'principle', insofar as it is this 'gathering', is precisely *lógos*, *legere*, *lex*. That is to say, the 'principle' is the *arché* that, as the Greek word itself clearly states, dominates and extends its domination to the point of reaching all things, including those that have already perished and those that have not yet been born. Philosophy's originary intention is certainly to reveal, manifest and exhibit the principle of all things; certainly, philosophy wants to be *theoría*: contemplation, vision. But precisely because *theoría* is a contemplation and vision of the immutable principle of all things, *theoría* is a prediction of the immutable order to which all things that arise in becoming must conform. It is for this reason that a pure *theoría* is equivalent to an absolute domination. Pure seeing is praxis: in fact, the most powerful form of praxis that could exist in the history of the West before the appearance of modern science. This is the case even if the essentially practical character of *theoría* remains hidden in the latter's own unconscious.

The immutable and eternal beings that the West has invoked in order to save itself – that is, in order to dominate the irruption of becoming – are, in turn, the god of the Greek-Christian tradition, the god of modern immanentism, the natural order and the natural law, the natural good and the natural beauty (which are mirrored in the righteous act and in the work of art), the immortal soul of human beings, the authority and the teachings of the 'Son of God' and of the Church, the authority of the master, of the monarch and of the State, the relations of production in the capitalist economy, the moral law, the determinism of nature, the dialectic rationality of history, the irreversibility of time, as well as communist society as outcome of the class struggle. At the origin of all the immutables stands the immutable being of the *epistéme*: namely, the locus – the

unwavering site – where every immutable can truthfully be
erected (and to which the absolutist conception of the empirical
and logico-mathematical sciences is directly connected). In this
first epoch of domination in the history of the West, the
immediate, familiar and everyday forms of domination – such as
dealing with the land, animals and humans – are experienced as
effective only insofar as they partake in the meaning of the world
opened by the invocation of the immutables; otherwise, they
appear as error, deviance or sin, and are inevitably doomed to fail.

IV

In the history of the West, however, the forms of domination that
precede the scientific one have an essentially antinomic character.
The antinomy lies in the fact that the immutable and eternal
beings, which are invoked by the epistemic prediction with the
aim of dominating becoming, render this very becoming
impossible and unthinkable. That is to say, they render impossible
what must be possible and thinkable in order to be dominated
– which is, in fact, what the West has regarded from the outset as
the most fundamental self-evidence.

If the becoming of the world is an extreme threat and origin
of anxiety for mortals, it is nevertheless inescapable. Becoming is
the fundamental self-evidence because it prominently belongs to
the content of the *epistéme*. Insofar as it is incontrovertible
knowledge, the *epistéme* is equivalent to an incontrovertible
assertion and vision of a content that includes the becoming of

the world. In fact, the vision of becoming belongs to the very ground on which the *epistéme* is established.

Therefore, the essentially antinomic character of the prescientific forms of domination also pertains – and, in fact, primarily – to the *epistéme*. The *epistéme* is invoked in order to dominate becoming, but it is the *epistéme* itself that renders becoming impossible – and, therefore, that renders itself impossible insofar as it supports the conviction that becoming should be the object of an incontrovertible vision.

The will to dominate becoming is the most radical acknowledgment of the existence of becoming itself (particularly if this will establishes itself as *epistéme*). But the domination of becoming by means of the invocation of the *epistéme*, and of the immutables that one after the other come to be erected within the *epistéme*, requires a meaning of the world that is incompatible with the existence of becoming itself. Why, then, are we claiming this?

V

Greek thought establishes, once and for all, the meaning of the becoming of the world. The whole of Western civilisation – including also, therefore, modern science, regarded both as empirical knowledge and as a logico-mathematical formalism – unfolds within the Greek meaning of becoming.

For Greek thought, the becoming of all things is equivalent to their emerging from and returning to nothingness – that is, their beginning and ceasing to be. Nothingness has nothing to do with any sort of empty space: a thing issues from nothingness in that, before being, it is no-thing at all – it is nothing. It issues from nothingness in the sense that, by beginning to be, it does not issue from any dimension: that is to say, it has nothing behind itself.

Certainly, the conditions of the thing already exist before the thing has come to be, and parts of the thing or the materials of which it is composed can already exist. For instance: before an amphora has come to be, the clay already exists – and so do the potter, the project that he intends to realise, the instruments he uses for the work, etc. Before the amphora has come to be, however, the amphora itself is not; and, to the extent that it is not, it is nothing. A thing, as it begins to be, issues from this very being-nothing [*esser niente*]. Most of what pertains to the amphora already exists (that is, it is not nothing) before the amphora has come to be. But the unity that gathers in itself everything that in this way preexists the amphora – and which makes it, precisely, an amphora (and, in fact, *this* amphora, *this* unity that the amphora as such is) – this specific and singular unity does not exist before the amphora has come to be.

While most of what pertains to the amphora can preexist the amphora itself, it cannot be *everything* that pertains to the amphora, or *everything* that the amphora is, that preexists the amphora itself. If *the whole* of a thing, which begins to be, preexisted the thing itself, it would not be possible to state that the thing begins to be: namely, it would not be possible to state that the thing becomes. What does not preexist the thing is the thing itself insofar as it begins to be. Everything that begins to be is nothing before this beginning.

Only starting with Greek philosophy has this nothingness been thought with regard to its infinite remove from beings: namely, as a *not-being-any* of the things (and, therefore, as a *not-being-any* of the aspects, the functions and the meanings of things). But it is precisely due to this radical character of nothingness that, at the beginning of Western civilisation, the threat of becoming becomes extreme.

In the history of mortals, the threat of becoming becomes extreme precisely when the Greek invocation of the immutables appears: this is the first decisive form of the domination of becoming enacted by the West. The irruption of becoming threatens existing things in that what irrupts is something new, unpredictable and unforeseen. But if the boundary between existence and that region, from which what irrupts into existence originates, remains blurred and uncertain – and if, as in myths, it remains unsettled where the domain of reality ends and where the realm of shadows, from which the threat of becoming irrupts, begins – then, the possibility always remains open of finding a path that, however hidden, would connect the world with what has not yet irrupted into it. This is a path that would somehow render predictable and familiar what, in fact, escapes the prediction only provisionally and as a matter of fact.

The Greek meaning of nothingness, however, makes it impossible precisely to traverse this path. For nothingness is, precisely, nothing; it does not contain anything, and, therefore, it does not contain anything that may be predicted and expected. But everything that, in becoming, irrupts into the world, and begins to be, issues from nothingness – it has been a nothingness. It is precisely by virtue of this having been a nothingness that what irrupts into the world is absolutely and infinitely unpredictable, unforeseen, new and unprecedented; and, therefore, that it is the most extreme threat for all existing things.

What issues from nothingness begins in an absolute way, without any tendencies, vocations, inclinations or propensities, without having any aims and without being subjected to any rules, laws or principles. It has nothing behind itself; its approaching the edge of existence is not entrusted to anything, it has nothing in view, it has no reasons or ends. Nothingness is nothing, and there cannot be a reason that would prompt it in one direction rather than in a different one. Everything that, in becoming, begins to be – precisely because it has been a nothingness – is pure *chance*. In the history of the West, the meaning of chance is indissolubly connected to the meaning of nothingness. In its essential meaning, chance is an emerging from nothingness: it is a falling upon existence without having been thrown by anything. Becoming is, in itself, chance. The so-called regularities, according to which all the things that begin to be are arranged, are just a fact: that is, these regularities themselves take place by chance.

This is the case even if Greek thought constantly avoids making the meaning it attributes to chance explicit, reducing it – as in Aristotle – to a particular kind of becoming (*gígnesthai apó túches*) that is subordinate with respect to becoming caused by nature or by art (*gígnesthai phúsei, téchnei*). What becomes by virtue of a human or divine *téchne* is certainly regarded as the realisation of an end; but, insofar as it becomes – that is, insofar as it issues from its having been a nothingness – its conformity to an end is only the external aspect of its radical lack of ends. That is, its very conformity to an end takes place by chance. In Greek, aside from *túche*, chance is designated by the word *autómaton*, which explicitly signifies – when the Greek language is spoken by the *epistéme* – the irruption of becoming (*máomai*) by way of something that is the sole protagonist and cause of this irruption: that is, something that irrupts 'by itself' (*autó*), while being or having nothing before this irruption.

VI

The sequence of events that leads the threat of becoming to reach an extreme form is the very sequence of events that leads to the first crucial form of domination accomplished by the West. This sequence of events consists in the Greek invocation of the immutables. It is indeed within the *epistéme* that the essential meaning of becoming, nothingness and chance is established. The West invokes all its immutables in order to dominate becoming insofar as it is thought and experienced in this essential meaning.

We have begun to explain, however, that the immutables – namely, the gods of the West – render the essential meaning that the West attributes to becoming impossible. The immutable is what is not threatened by any becoming. It stands always and forever outside of nothingness, 'always saved' as Aristotle says (*os tês toiaútes phúseos aieì sozoménes*, *Metaphysics*: 983b, 12–13). Since no becoming can overthrow it, and since no novelty can irrupt that may surprise it and force it to yield, the immutable divests becoming of any unpredictability. That is to say, the immutable is the *law* to which everything that arises must submit. Precisely in the same way in which an unassailable fortress is not simply a defensive structure, but rather extends its domination everywhere – since also those in the remotest districts know that they will never overthrow it, and, therefore, they adjust their existence according to this awareness – so not only does the immutable close ranks around the existence of everything, but forces every event to conform to its nature.

The meaning of existence introduced by the immutable – and which constitutes the immutable – has no limits; it reaches even the farthest districts of what is still a nothingness, and there it dictates its law: even everything that is still a nothingness will have to conform, by beginning to be, to the law of the immutable. In fact, everything that is still a nothingness has already conformed to this law: it is already subjected to the law that dictates that, when it begins to exist, it will have to conform to the law of existence. But if the law reaches nothingness itself, and dictates to it its meaning – if nothingness is no longer unpredictable, since nothing can issue from it that would escape this law – then, nothingness is no longer a nothingness, but has turned into one of the regions that are ruled by the law of the immutable. And if nothingness is no longer nothingness, the emerging of things from nothingness, namely the becoming of the world, becomes a mere appearance.

Effectively, the immutable has already predicted and anticipated everything in itself. There is no longer any room for a real becoming of the world: *both* as the immutable comes forward in the form of the god of the Greek-Christian tradition, of the relations of production regarded by the paleo-capitalist economy as natural laws, of the deterministic order of the universe, of the necessary overcoming of the contradiction of capitalism in the communist society; *and*, particularly, as the immutable comes forward in the form of philosophy *qua* *epistéme*: that is to say, as the definitive and incontrovertible truth within which there emerges the meaning to which everything – in the heavens, on earth, and in the Hades of nothingness – must conform.

The immutable predicts, anticipates and dominates the becoming of the world by establishing its own law: but this domination renders impossible and unthinkable what it is supposed to dominate. The law of the immutable prevents nothingness from being nothing, chance from being chance, becoming from being becoming. And yet, this law has been invoked precisely in order to save from what is regarded as the most real and inescapable reality: becoming – namely, the be-falling [*ac-cadere*] of events that issue from their own nothingness. This is the antinomic character of the immutables: that is, of the gods of the West.

VII

Becoming, however, as the process of issuing from and returning to nothingness, is also the originary self-evidence that, since the Greek *epistéme*, has not been put into question in the history of the West – not even when modern science and certain forms of contemporary philosophy believe it to be possible to completely leave the Greek meaning of becoming out of account.

The existence of becoming is the originary self-evidence of the West, and the West invokes the immutables precisely in order to dominate becoming. By means of the invocation of the immutables, this form of domination ends up erasing becoming on the grounds of the most categorical acknowledgment of the existence of becoming itself. It is therefore unavoidable that this form of domination should end up exhibiting its oneiric character, as well as, therefore, its lack of power against those events that, in arising, tear the fabric of the immutables apart. These are the events that irrupt into existence as a radical novelty and unpredictability – and, therefore, in the form of an extreme and incessant threat. In order to truly dominate becoming, it is therefore necessary to break the spell of the immutables – the dream within which it is possible to dominate only by turning one's back on what, in fact, is meant to be dominated. Meta-physics is equivalent, precisely, to the *epistéme* that, starting with *phúsis* – namely, with the self-evidence of becoming – moves beyond becoming by invoking the dimension of the immutables. Metaphysics is, precisely, a dreamt domination [*dominio sognato*].

Therefore, the will to power demands the destruction of the immutables because it is necessarily linked to the faith in the existence of what this power itself must act upon. That is, the will to power is necessarily linked to the faith in the existence of becoming – an existence that is irreconcilable with the existence of the immutables. The history of the West, as history of the extreme form of the will to power, is the history of the invocation and destruction of the immutables.

This destruction ranges from the destruction of god and of the universal concept – which anticipates in itself every individuation, in the same way in which god anticipates in itself every event of the world – to the destruction of tonality in musical languages, and of every 'natural form' in the work of art; from the destruction of the capitalist relations of production to the destruction of the author and of the written text in Artaud's 'theatre of cruelty'; it is equivalent to the very destruction of traditional civilisation and of its values. The force that destructs this tradition, however, coincides with the very essence of this tradition – namely, with the will to dominate becoming. Therefore, this will comes to contradict the form that the tradition has imparted to its own essence by means of the invocation of the immutables. The destruction is unavoidable.

This unavoidability is to be sought, however, below the level on which the culture of the West becomes aware of the destruction of the immutables. The West is completely immersed in the Greek meaning of becoming; but, precisely for this reason, the West cannot bring this meaning to the fore. It is, however, precisely and exclusively the Greek meaning of becoming that entails, *necessarily*, the impossibility of the immutables, as well as of the cultural forms that are founded upon them. If the Greek meaning of becoming is not brought to the fore, the *unavoidability* of the destruction of the immutables cannot come into view. As a result, this destruction appears, within Western culture, as a mere fact that is, as such, constantly exposed to the possibility of revision.

All the critiques that contemporary culture and civilisation direct at the culture and at the civilisation of the Western tradition only constitute an attempt at the destruction of the immutables – for they are only an epiphenomenon of the essential destruction that takes place in an underground that is permeated with the Greek meaning of becoming.

From Epistemic to Scientific Domination

VIII

Modern science is the decisive force that, in the history of the West, drives towards the destruction of the immutables. Which is to say that, through science, the domination of becoming reaches its most radical form. Outside of the spell, within which the immutables dissolve becoming, scientific predictions succeed in 'truly' dominating becoming.

This actual domination is made possible by the experimental character of science. According to this character, the value of a prediction is not determined by the immutable meaning of the totality through which the *epistéme* anticipates everything that can arise: it is rather experience that decides, in the last instance, the value of every prediction – and experience does not let predictions obtain a definitive and incontrovertible value.

Science becomes the most powerful form of domination because it relinquishes the epistemic dream of an incontrovertible prediction, thereby becoming a hypothetical prediction that is, as such, always open to the risk of failure. Contemporary culture has, by now, acquired a thorough awareness of the hypothetical character of science, as well as of its extreme possibilities of domination. What, instead, keeps being overlooked is that modern science is the most powerful form of domination because it is the one that best conforms to the Greek meaning of becoming: namely, it is the form of domination in which the Greek meaning of becoming is present with a coherence and an intensity that had never been attained before.

Experience does not merely let what begins to be irrupt – but rather welcomes it in order to put it to trial. To welcome the event means to observe it: not in order to allow it to come forth, but in order to try it out. The Latin word *experientia*, and the corresponding Greek word *peîra* (from which *empeiría*), mean precisely 'trial' ['*prova*']. What begins to be is put to trial in the sense that one tries to predict from the ground that it provides: that is, one tries to adopt it as a repository that provides – more or less directly – the content of the prediction. The trial has no guaranteed outcome; to try means to be exposed to a danger: the Latin word *periculum* is constructed on the same root of *experientia* and of *peîra*. Experience – and, therefore, the whole edifice of scientific knowledge to which it is connected – never ceases to be a trial. No matter how good the so-called 'confirmation' of a trial is, the possibility of failing the trial always remains open: namely, it is always possible that something might irrupt and appear as a novelty that is completely irreducible to what has been predicted.

By now, scientific knowledge is fully aware that the possibility of the irruption of an unpredictable novelty is not linked to an increase in the confirmation of the trial: therefore, this possibility is in no way reduced or weakened by an indefinite increase in the confirmation. The possibility of an irruption of the unforeseen is absolute. This possibility, however, can be absolute only because everything that begins to be is not – before this very beginning – something: it is nothing, and as such a nothingness it is not something that can be subjected to a prediction. As it begins to be, the event is free of all ties, and can therefore be the most radical refutation of the most confirmed prediction.

The possibility of an irruption of the unforeseen is absolute: namely, it is not linked to an increase in the confirmation. This is the case precisely according to the standpoint (Reichenbach) that posits the *probability* of a prediction as a function of the increase in the confirmation. The *continuum* that is established by this function has limit-values 1 and 0; they are limit values – namely, they are unattainable – because 1 indicates a logical implication (regarded as a tautology) and 0 indicates the negation of this implication (namely, a contradiction). In the scientific interpretation of logic, neither of these can constitute a statement that refers to experience. Stating that 1 is the upper limit of the probability function – namely, stating that the certainty of the logical implication is unattainable by a prediction – means that, regardless of the proximity to 1 of the value of the probability of a prediction, the possibility of an irruption of the unforeseen remains unaltered. That is, absolute.

IX

It is not only the unforeseen event, which falsifies a certain degree of confirmation of the trial, that is free of all ties, but so are all the events that have contributed to the establishment of that degree. Each of these events is indeed a beginning to be: before this beginning, however, each of these events is a nothingness that is absolutely unpredictable – and, therefore, beyond the reach of any tie. The verification of the existence of the events that confirm the trial is not the verification of the existence of a connection – namely, of a law to which these events would be subjected. This is the case if by 'law' one understands something more than the pure arising of a series of events that are interpreted as the confirmation of a trial – namely, if by 'law' one understands the *inevitable* arising of this series.

Indeed, a series does not become inevitable as a result of its occurrence. Each term of the series could have not arisen: by verifying a certain degree of confirmation of the trial, it is not thereby known that a trial has not been a trial – namely, an openness to the possibility of the unforeseen and of failure. That is to say, the series of events confirming a trial is a pure fact, which has a certain configuration but could have had a different one, and which could have also altogether not existed. The existence and the configuration of a series are pure occurrences; they are, precisely, chance.

Since an 'empirical regularity' is, precisely, a series of events that confirms the trial, *every* empirical regularity takes place purely by chance. That is to say, a regularity consists in nothing but in the simple fact that all terms of a series can be interpreted as a confirmation of the trial.

If a rule necessarily determined what is to arise, an epistemic prediction of the succession would have to be possible as a matter of principle. This prediction is, on the contrary, impossible precisely as a matter of principle (and not primarily due to the Humean critique of the inductive process). The Humean critique is valid in that it presupposes the impossibility of a synthetic *a priori* knowledge: in the Humean perspective, however, this remains a presupposition, namely an assertion devoid of an absolute foundation. It is an assertion that cannot be synthetic *a priori*: therefore – since neither is it a tautology – it can only assert the absence of a synthetic *a priori* knowledge *de facto* but not *de jure*. An epistemic prediction is impossible *de jure* because it is impossible to predict anything of nothingness – of the nothingness that every event is before beginning to be. It is on the hidden ground of the impossibility of predicting anything of nothingness that the empiricist refutation of a synthetic *a priori* knowledge attains all its strength.

Indeed, synthetic *a priori* knowledge expresses the very contradiction of the *epistéme*: insofar as it is synthetic, it connects what exists to its other – namely, to what does not yet exist, to nothingness; insofar as it is *a priori*, it establishes in advance and it anticipates in itself the behaviour of what is still a nothingness – thereby transforming nothingness in a being, and thus erasing becoming. Nothingness is unpredictable: therefore, the only kind of prediction that is possible is a hypothetical one. This kind of prediction obtains, as a matter of fact, a greater degree

of confirmation if it attempts to regard what has taken place
in certain conditions as being similar to what will take place
in similar ones. A hypothesis does not dictate any law to
nothingness, but rather adapts its own content to the
confirmation of what arises from nothingness – a confirmation
that takes place by chance. In this way, the two components of
the *a priori* synthesis come apart: while the synthetic component
acquires a hypothetical character, the epistemic absoluteness
of the *a priori* component becomes the simple absoluteness of
the tautology of analytic logic – namely, the absoluteness that
expresses the simple conformity of a proposition to the rules
for using the words of which it is composed.

X

It is precisely on the basis of the hidden ground of the
unpredictability of nothingness that the frequentist theory of
probability inevitably extends its original domain of applicability
– that particular domain constituted by the series of events that
fulfil the definition of 'collective' provided by von Mises – up to
the point of controlling the totality of events. As a result, every
single thing of the world becomes a rolling die, and the whole
science of nature becomes the probabilistic and statistical
prediction of the outcomes of a game.

Indeed, in a series of events – which confirm a prediction, and
which, therefore, do not form a 'collective' as to their regular
distribution – a regularity takes place purely by chance. This is

the case because every event, in issuing from nothingness, is not compelled to be submitted to any rules. Which does not mean that it is not possible to distinguish the series that are regarded as being regular from those that take place by chance (such as 'collectives'); it means that the laws that express the regular series are forms or outcomes of chance [*casi del caso*]. In modern science, the transformation of causal laws into probabilistic ones is a transformation into laws that, precisely, express the frequency of those events that confirm a certain prediction by chance.

However, putting to trial the capacity of the event to deliver the content of a prediction – scientific inductions, which have freed themselves from any epistemic residue, consist precisely in this trying out – is already equivalent, in its essence, to that reference to the taking place by chance of the event (and, in fact, of any event) that becomes explicit in the theory of probability. Precisely for this reason, scientific inductions are, in their essence, already equivalent to that indeterminism that becomes explicit in contemporary physics with Heisenberg's indeterminacy principle. In the same way in which, for quantum theory, the state of a physical system at a certain instant in time is not necessarily determined by the previous instant, so in an inductive process the state constituted by a certain degree of confirmation of the trial does not necessarily determine the subsequent degree of confirmation of that same trial. The latter is the degree that is established in relation to the emerging of a new confirming element (in such a way that the prediction of the subsequent degree of confirmation has already that probabilistic character, which is made explicit in the prediction of the quantities of the subsequent state of the physical system).

XI

The *epistéme* does not succeed in dominating because the unpredictable novelty of what begins to be tears apart the immutable mesh thrown by the prediction of the *epistéme* on the becoming of the world. Scientific predictions succeed because they are first of all equivalent, in their hidden essence, to the acknowledgement of the unpredictability and novelty of what begins to be. Which is to say, they are equivalent to the acknowledgement that the event arises from nothingness, and that, in its being nothing, it is absolutely unpredictable. Scientific predictions, precisely because they are equivalent to this acknowledgement, destroy, by means of their content, every immutable, and try to anticipate non-existing events by means of existing ones. That is to say, they try to take advantage of the event in order to enmesh the event itself, and to take advantage of the known aspects of what takes place by chance in order to guess those that do not yet exist. The very success of a trial takes place by chance (that is, the long sequences of empirical regularities that confirm the trials carried out by science take place by chance). But precisely because the *epistéme* renders chance impossible, it renders success impossible: that is to say, the domination realised by the *epistéme* appears like a dream that lets itself be swept away by chance.

All of this has nothing to do with a sort of reactionary or romantic repudiation of scientific rationality. The form of rationality realised by modern science is the most rigorous one among those grounded in the faith in the becoming of the world (this faith grounds, starting with the Greeks, the whole history of the West). This is the case because, on the ground of this faith, any incontrovertible truth is impossible, and 'reason' can only consist in a power for domination – whereas every form of 'reason' brought forth by traditional culture finds itself powerless in front of the dominion of science and technics.

It is precisely because science recognises that it is not itself *epistéme* – that is, incontrovertible truth and invocation of the immutables – that it could be-fall [*ac-cadere*] science to be the most powerful form of domination, and, therefore, the highest form of rationality: namely, that could befall science what could not befall the immutables of the *epistéme*. That it could befall science to be the highest form of domination and rationality means precisely that the existence of domination, as well as the existence of the success of the trial, takes place by chance – and so does the existence of rationality. But, once again, if the success of scientific trials is a matter of chance (namely, of a be-fallen [*un ac-caduto*]), this chance can befall only on the condition that the spell of the immutables, which make this befalling impossible, be destroyed.

The Greek Meaning of Nothingness in Modern Science

XII

The twilight of the *epistéme* erases every discontinuity between science and the critical reflection on science itself. This reflection becomes the comprehension that the will to power has of itself insofar as it is a scientific undertaking. In the scientific domain, however, the *epistéme* reaches its twilight through a process that continues to this day. The inductive procedure itself has preserved for a long time some of the characteristic traits of the *epistéme* – in particular for what concerns the matter of understanding the 'datum' ['*dato*'] of experience.

'Datum' means both the event that experience puts to trial, as well as the event that constitutes the success or failure of the trial.

But modern science, since its beginning, has considered this datum not only as something that is given [*dato*] 'to me', but as something that, under determinate conditions, 'everyone else' is able to recognise. The possibility of being recognised by other people is, in fact, an essential component of a datum, and it is in relation to this component that what is given 'to me' comes to be constituted. And not vice-versa: for if 'my' data do not enjoy a social consensus, then I have to be ready, from the very standpoint of the scientific activity, to acknowledge a dysfunction of my mental and sensory apparatus.

Indeed, science claims to be able to operate a transformation of the world only if the event, in which this transformation consists, is not simply something that is given to me, but is the object of a recognition by others – which is to say, only if this recognition is a datum. Accordingly, from the standpoint of science, the datum, insofar as it is 'given [*dato*] to me', is only a part of the datum that also includes the social consensus, or lack thereof, with respect to what is given to me. In turn, the data that afford the structure of predictions, which is at the basis of a certain practical transformation of the world, have a scientific value only if they enjoy the consensus of a community of researchers. Science primarily appears, even from its own standpoint, as an intersubjective language in which a social consensus is expressed not only with respect to what is given 'to me' (or 'to an I', or 'to someone'), but also with respect to contents that have not, as of yet, constituted a datum for me, and to contents that perhaps never will.

But it is in a neo-positivist milieu, and within the echo of the Kantian notion of objectivity as intersubjectivity, that the critical reflection on science makes the intersubjective and linguistic character of the datum completely explicit. In its external form, this process appears (in Neurath, Popper, Reininger, Carnap, Reichenbach) as a refutation of the absolute value of those statements that refer to empirical data ('protocol statements') – an absolute value that, however, had been affirmed in the initial phase of neo-positivism (by Wittgenstein, Schlick and Carnap himself).

Protocol statements – in particular in the form in which they express quantified spatio-temporal data – certainly enjoy the highest degree of intersubjective consensus as compared to all other scientific statements; accordingly, they serve as foundation for the entirety of the linguistic edifice of science. However, this consensus and this role of foundation are merely a fact (namely, a situation that is provisional and, therefore, variable): they do not follow from the alleged absolute value of statements referring to empirical data. These latter statements, on the other hand, can in turn be considered as trials – namely, as theories that must be tested – thereby serving as foundation only by virtue of the *decision* not to involve them in the process of testing.

Popper has established an analogy between the acceptance of protocol statements and the verdict with which, in a certain kind of juridical trials, the jury decides to accept a statement affirming the occurrence of a certain fact. Protocol statements serve as foundation for both the theoretical system of science and for its application to the empirical datum, to the same extent to which the verdict of a jury serves as foundation for the application of the system of legislation that is in force. A verdict is a decision that acts in response to a question posed by the law that is in force, in such a way that the verdict that affords the application of the juridical system is itself an application of that very system. In the same way, the acceptance of the statements referring to the empirical datum is not an absolute and independent foundation of a scientific theory, but a decision that is produced within the application of a part of that same scientific theory that has, as a whole, protocol statements as its foundation. It is a verdict – namely, a social consensus – that establishes which statements express the datum.

Beyond the boundaries of neo-positivism, the indication of the essential affinity between the intersubjective character of modern science and the democratic principle of the will of the majority of the people (Bakunin, Dietzgen, Sombart, Scheler) was already at work. Indeed, the absolute character of what is 'given to me' stands in relation to the intersubjective consensus in the same way in which an absolute monarch stands in relation to the consensus of the subjects: it is the datum and the absolute monarch that decide the value of the consensus, or possible lack thereof. They are the immutables that render the becoming of the consensus impossible. (From the perspective of the absolute character of the datum, the fact that this spot of colour should effectively be, in itself, the way I see it is a statement that will remain true forever, even when the spot no longer exists. Equivalently, that justice and the good should coincide with the will of the monarch remains an eternal truth independently of the very existence of the monarch).

However, the dominion established by the consensus is revealed to be powerless, for the unpredictable way in which a lack of consensus can occur overthrows the monarch and insinuates a doubt into the certainties of the single person as to the world that is given to them. What is 'given to me', not unlike the moral law, must be accepted even if this leads to the most radical practical failure. The moral law and the epistemic concept of the datum, however, reward the failure in the world with a domination in what is regarded as the 'true' dimension of existence.

When science unmasks the oneiric character of this domination, it becomes necessary to also put into question the absolute character of the datum. In particular for what concerns the will to domination, wherein science consists, success is equivalent to the capacity for predicting those events whose existence can be intersubjectively recognised. On the other hand, the assertion of the absolute value of what is given to the consciousness of a single person subordinates the intersubjective conduct to this datum, thereby rendering a real domination impossible. It was therefore inevitable that the methodology of science would come to the refutation of the absolute value of the statements that refer to the empirical datum. Beneath the external form of this repudiation, however, the destruction of the immutables, which is accomplished by the faith in the Greek meaning of becoming, is at work. Scientific inductions, contrary to epistemic predictions, are hypothetical predictions that do not render the very becoming, which they want to dominate, impossible. For the data that are put to trial in a scientific induction, and which confirm the trial itself, have an intersubjective, and therefore provisional character: that is, their acknowledgement depends on an intersubjective consensus that exists only as a matter of fact. The success of scientific predictions takes place in relation to a datum that is understood in this sense. However, if the datum that appears in the inductive procedure is regarded as an absolute one – insofar as it is 'given to me' – then it can no longer functionally be part of the dimension of intersubjectivity: and, therefore, of the real domination (precisely because, insofar as it is absolute, it is not subordinate to the social consensus, but subordinates the latter to itself). Accordingly, the absolute datum relinquishes its inclusion in a dimension of intersubjectivity because it presents itself as an epistemic prediction of becoming: namely, as an immutable that anticipates in itself the value of every possible intersubjective conduct that could concern it. By means of this anticipation, the absolute datum entifies [*entifica*] what is still a nothingness, thereby preventing the social practice that confirms the prediction from constituting an event – namely, an emerging from nothingness. The will to truly dominate becoming, by returning to the event its own character of event, is also at work at the foundation of the critique of the absolute value of protocol statements.

XIII

It is, however, once again a critique of the absolute value of the datum – namely, of the absolute value of intuition or of the certainty of intuitive meanings – that determines the radical transformation of modern geometry, mathematics, and logic into formal axiomatic systems. The rules of formation and transformation of these systems no longer express an intuitive certainty, for they rather posit themselves as conventions: namely, as decisions taken within an intersubjective consensus.

The absolute character of the intuition of Euclidean space renders impossible the novelty – which is, incidentally, actual and irreducible – introduced by those conceptual determinations of non-Euclidean geometries that render the Euclidean intuition of space self-contradictory. In the same way, the intuitive absolute character of the mathematical notion of 'set' is not able to contain the irruption of the novelty constituted by the antinomies that unpredictably arise from that very notion. The absolute character of an intuitive meaning is not able to control and resolve the contradictions that unpredictably originate from within itself.

In the construction of formal systems, contradictions are explicitly recognised for what concerns their character of radical unpredictability – that is to say, they are recognised as something whose emergence cannot be *a priori* excluded by the seeming coherence of the rules of formation and transformation of the formal axiomatic system. Hilbert's attempt at demonstrating the non-contradictory nature of the axiomatic system that formalises arithmetic fails as Gödel demonstrates the impossibility of operating such a control of contradictions based on the rules of formation and transformation of the system. It is not only in relation to the theoretical apparatus of the empirical sciences that the absolute unpredictability of the event introduces a contradiction in the theory; the theoretical apparatus of the logico-mathematical formalisms is also open to the irruption of a conceptual event that determines the contradiction of the formalism. Gödel's cultural operation is directed against the ambition of formal systems to be able to warrant against the emergence of contradictions. In this respect, it is analogous not only to the operation by means of which the empirical sciences hold themselves open to the novelty of the event, but also to the operation through which both Marxism and neo-capitalism (Weber, Schumpeter, Keynes) come to regard the capitalist economic order as a system that is not absolute, but rather open to the irruption of an unpredictable social event that would make the contradiction of the system explode.

The destruction of the immutables accomplished by the unpredictable novelty of the event is precisely determined by the contradiction introduced by the event in the immutable structure. The event irrupts into this structure precisely as an unpredictable novelty that contradicts the very dimension that, by transforming the originary nothingness of the event into a non-nothingness [*un non niente*], aims to anticipate it and reduce it to itself. Gödel's theorem demonstrates the unpredictability of the contradiction in a formal axiomatic system of a sufficient complexity by demonstrating the undecidability of the proposition that, within that system, states the non-contradictory nature of the system itself. In this respect, Gödel's theorem plays the same role as Planck's constant, insofar as the latter establishes, in the probabilistic predictions of quantum physics, the limit of precision in the measurement of 'conjugate' quantities.

As in the empirical sciences, the scientific character of the theoretical construction that takes place within the logico-mathematical formalisms is once again determined by an intersubjective consensus. The conceptual determinations of mathematics and logic have been translated into a 'calculus': namely, into an empirical operation that, on the basis of certain operational rules, is performed on those empirical events represented by the physical signs of the calculus. The reason for this transformation – a transformation, that is, of the conceptual and logico-mathematical meaning into the empirical fact of the sequences of signs of the calculus – is given precisely by the fact that an intersubjective consensus is produced in relation to the calculus *qua* empirical fact, rather than in relation to a conceptual meaning *qua* distinct from the calculus. This reduction of meaning to the symbolism of empirical signs certainly constitutes the fundamental purpose of Hilbert's metamathematics; but it is highly operative also in those junctures of the history of logic, such as in G. Frege's *Begriffsschrift*, where the presence of the *epistéme* still plays a crucial role. Formalisms, by being reduced to a handling of physical signs, become a type of 'datum', which is analogous – first of all for what concerns its intersubjective character – to the datum of the empirical sciences.

XIV

The central position that the concept of probability has reached in contemporary science is the result of a process that – precisely insofar as it follows from an ever more rigorous application of the experimental method – reflects in itself the history of the invocation and destruction of the immutable beings.

Bernoullli's *Ars conjectandi* explicitly presents itself, as per its own title, as a prediction (*conjectura*, from *cum-jacio*: to throw ahead by means of a tool that allows the user to reach what stands in front): in particular, as a prediction of events that, like the ones that take place in gambling, cannot be reached by the *epistéme*. The prediction of these events is, therefore, the work of an *ars*: namely, an activity that is governed by rules that do not claim to stand as incontrovertible truths.

However, the essence of the critique, directed at the classical theory of probability from the standpoint of the frequentist theory, lies in the fact that the foundation of the classical theory is not the rule of an *ars*, but a law of the *epistéme*. In this critique, it is indeed emphasised that the 'principle of insufficient reason', or 'principle of indifference' (on the basis of which, in the classical theory, probability is defined as the ratio between the number of favourable outcomes and the number of possible ones), is a principle that is valid *a priori* – namely, a principle of logic – and, at the same time, it is an instrument of prediction – namely, it has a *synthetic* function. Therefore, it is a synthetic *a priori* principle. The *epistéme* is precisely the synthesis that traces every possible novelty back to the immutable meaning of what already exists, thereby linking every novelty to that meaning: in such a way that this unity or synthesis is *a priori* with respect to the arising of what is still a nothingness.

XV

It is possible, however, to proceed even further, and show in a determinate way the mechanism that transforms the principle of indifference into a synthetic *a priori* principle. The principle of indifference states that if, in a sufficiently determined situation (for instance, the one constituted by a throw of dice), no reason is known as to why an event should take place rather than a different one, then these events are 'equally likely' ['*equipossibili*'].

The notion 'equally likely', however, cannot refer to possibility as such: possible is that whose content is not self-contradictory, and something cannot be more (or less) free of contradiction, as would in fact be required by the notion 'equally likely' when referring to possibility as such. Something is either possible or not possible: possibility itself cannot be quantified.

Stating that two events are equally likely means, then, referring to *the way* in which what is possible can be realised. What can be quantified in the mode of realisation of the possible is the set of outcomes that are available to each possible event for its realisation – and which, therefore, are called 'favourable outcomes'. The possible event represented by a 'six', which appears when the die has come to a still, has at its disposal for its realisation that sole outcome that consists in the die having a single face with the number 'six'. If the adverb 'equally', in the notion 'equally likely', cannot refer to possibility as such, but only to what can be quantified in the mode of realisation of the possible (namely, to the number of favourable outcomes), then stating that two events are equally likely means that the same number of available outcomes is available to both of them.

Accordingly, the principle of indifference states that if one does not know any reason why one event should be realised rather than another, then the same number of favourable outcomes is available to each of these events.

This proposition is analytic only if it presupposes that, if a different number of favourable outcomes is available for the realisation of two possible events, then this would constitute a reason for asserting the realisation of the event for which more favourable outcomes are available, rather than the realisation of the other one. *If* having a greater number of favourable outcomes at its disposal is considered to be a reason for the realisation of the event that holds this greater number of favourable outcomes, rather than the event that holds the lesser number, then the following proposition is certainly analytic: 'If no reason is known why one event should take place rather than a different event, then the same number of favourable outcomes is available to each of these events'. The fact that having a greater number of favourable outcomes available should constitute a reason for the realisation of the event that holds this greater number, however, is only a hypothesis. For nothing excludes that, as a matter of fact, it should be precisely the events that hold a lesser number of favourable outcomes that come to constantly be realised – in such a way that, for instance, all (non-loaded) dice should come, at each throw, to always present the same face rather than any of the remaining five.

In the classical theory of probability, the analytic character of the inference constituting the principle of indifference comes to be covertly attributed to an implicit component of the antecedent of that inference: namely, to that component that consists precisely in the hypothesis that having favourable and available outcomes should constitute a reason for the realisation of an event. And, in fact, the greater the number of favourable outcomes, the stronger this reason would be. If, indeed, having favourable and available outcomes is considered to constitute a reason for the realisation of the possible event that has these outcomes at its disposal, then having a greater number of favourable and available outcomes is considered to constitute a reason for the realisation of the event that holds this greater number of outcomes (rather than the event that holds the lesser number). And since probability, in the classical theory, is nothing but the ratio between the number of favourable outcomes and the number of events that, in a determinate context, are considered to be possible, it follows that the probability of an event comes to be considered as a reason for its realisation.

Therefore, the statement, which affirms that the probability for a die to show a 'five' is one sixth, becomes an analytic proposition in the classical theory. For it covertly expresses this other proposition: 'If no reason is known as to why a "five" should appear, rather than any other face of the die – other than the reason that the "five" has one outcome out of six available for its realisation – then the probability that a "five" should appear is one sixth'. This proposition is certainly analytic; whereas it is only a hypothesis that the probability of an event should constitute a reason for its realisation, or that the greater probability of an event, as compared to a second one, should constitute a reason for the realisation of the first one, rather than the second one. An analytic character is here, once again, covertly attributed to this hypothesis: an analytic character that belongs to the inference whose antecedent has that hypothesis as a component. It is precisely because of this covert attribution of analyticity to the hypothesis that is implicitly included in the principle of indifference, as well as in the probabilistic statements that are grounded on it, that this principle and these statements come to appear as *a priori* syntheses.

XVI

In the development of the theory of probability, the part of the principle of indifference that has been rejected is precisely the attempt at attributing an analytic value to the mentioned hypothesis, thereby transforming it into a synthetic *a priori* principle. The heuristic value of this hypothesis, however, has not been rejected – in the sense that this hypothesis has been used as a prediction that has received extensive confirmation by the empirical observation of the relative frequencies of the possible events. Furthermore, the very quantification of the ratio between favourable outcomes and possible ones has been regarded, in turn, as a result of the observation of the relative frequencies.

The critique directed at the frequentist notion of probability – *qua* limit of the relative frequencies in a 'collective' (that is, in an infinitely increasing series) – essentially expresses the rejection of the epistemic character of the application of the mathematical notion of limit to the irregularity of a statistical series. In the same way, however, in which the epistemic character of the principle of indifference, but not its heuristic value, has been rejected, so that critique does not express a rejection of the heuristic value of that application.

A sequence that takes place by chance undoubtedly lacks any law of formation; the mathematical notion of a limit of a sequence, however, is precisely a law for the formation of that sequence. That the terms of a mathematical sequence should obey the conditions indicated by the law of formation of that sequence is an analytic proposition. That is to say, the terms of a mathematical sequence do not constitute any novelty with respect to the law that generates their succession (and, strictly speaking, this succession is not a becoming but a simple repetition). However, if the terms of a statistical sequence – namely, of a sequence that constitutes an authentic becoming – obey a law of formation, then the *a priori* character of this law anticipates in itself the unpredictability and novelty of the terms of the statistical sequence – thereby eliminating every element of chance from the sequence. As a result, the very application of the notion of limit to the statistical sequence becomes, in turn, an epistemic principle – namely, a synthetic *a priori* law: synthetic, insofar as it aims to preserve the difference between the predictability of the mathematical series and the unpredictability of the statistical one; *a priori*, insofar as it nevertheless aims to control the unpredictability of the statistical series.

The contradiction, mathematically considered, of the application of the mathematical notion of limit to a series that does not obey any law of formation implicitly expresses the impossibility that the nothingness, out of which the terms of the statistical series emerge, should be accountable to a law that anticipates it and pre-determines it. As a result, this nothingness, which has thus been ac-counted for [*contato*], is transformed into a non-nothingness [*un non-niente*]. This is the same transformation that – implicitly – is aimed to be avoided when, through the refutation of the epistemic value of the principle of indifference, the possibility is upheld that the probability of an event could come to appear, in the actual becoming of the events, as being different from what is pre-determined by that principle. In the same way, however, the application of the mathematical notion of limit is no longer a synthetic *a priori* principle if it is regarded as a heuristic hypothesis: one that, on the basis of the observation of the emergence of a certain constant percentage – which is, precisely, the limit of the observed sequence – advances the prediction that the sequence will converge to this limit in its further progress.

(Popper calls 'the fundamental problem of the theory of chance' the paradox that consists in the application of the calculus of probability to sequences of events that take place by chance and that are therefore incalculable. Analogously to what has been said so far, albeit in a considerably different theoretical context – which, incidentally, eliminates the 'axiom of convergence' – Popper solves this problem by attributing the value of 'frequency *hypothesis*' to the 'axiom of disorder', which, for von Mises, has the task of determining the conditions of chance and disorder by means of a mathematical law.)

XVII

Every inductive inference is a probabilistic one: namely, it consists in the observation of the relative frequency with which the terms of a sequence, to which a certain property belongs, appear together with a certain other property. It is once again an inductive inference that determines the limit of a frequency by attributing to it a numerical value – which remains, therefore, open to potential deviations of the sequence. And it is precisely because of the absolute unpredictability of a becoming that issues from nothingness that the theory of probability can recognise that the distinction between ordered and disordered sequences (and, therefore, between causal and probabilistic laws) is absolutely provisional and conventional. It justifies this recognition by stating that the longest of the observed ordered sequences could be the smallest segment of a long disordered sequence (in which that segment would be subjected to a so-called probabilistic distribution: namely, it would appear on average with the same frequency as other segments constituted by variously ordered or disordered sequences). And, vice-versa, the longest of the observed disordered sequences could be the smallest segment of an ordered sequence. Quantum physics does nothing but reaffirm the conventional character of the distinction between causal and probabilistic laws.

Law and chance, as they appear in the theory of probability, are two aspects of chance insofar as this is a be-falling that falls out of nothingness [*un accadere che cade da niente*]. In this respect, every scientific law (be that causal or probabilistic) is a law of chance; and this is not a paradox that ought to disappear through an analysis of language, but it is the situation in which the will to power must find itself in order to be able to dominate becoming without deceptively erasing it.

XVIII

The best-known aspect of quantum physics is the refutation of determinism – a refutation that is based on the principle of indeterminacy. Modern science inherits determinism from the *epistéme* as an immutable – one by which it lets itself be guided for the longest time.

In quantum physics, however, the destruction of determinism is accomplished only by means of the elimination of the subjectivist interpretation of the principle of indeterminacy. This interpretation recognises the structural difference between the application of probabilistic laws in a context such as the one of the kinetic theory of gases and the application of these laws to quantum mechanics. That is to say, it recognises that the limit in the precision of the measurement of 'conjugate' quantities is not ascribable to the provisional imperfection of the instruments, but expresses a fundamental law of quantum mechanics. And yet, in turn, it interprets this law as the expression of a constitutive limit of human knowledge, which would be unable to grasp the deterministic order of nature. On the contrary, the principle of indeterminacy leads not only to the refutation of the possibility of knowing the deterministic order, but to the refutation of its very existence. In the same way in which determinism is essentially connected to the predictability of the future state of the world, the principle of indeterminacy is essentially connected to the unpredictability of this state. In the principle of indeterminacy, the unpredictability of the event seemingly appears as a *consequence* of the impossibility of a simultaneous measurement of the position and velocity of a particle. The *fundamental* faith of the West – the faith in the existence of becoming; that is, in the absolute unpredictability of the event – seems to appear here as a consequence, or as a result, of the experimental situation determined by the behaviour of particles with respect to the radiation by which they are illuminated. However, why does the non-subjectivist interpretation of the principle of indeterminacy emerge among the very theorists of quantum mechanics – in particular in Heisenberg and Bohr (and concurrently in M. Schlick)? This is the interpretation according to which the simultaneous ratio between position and velocity of a particle is not a reality that is in itself unknowable, but something that, as a matter of principle, cannot be observed, and which is therefore a meaningless expression. Why does the neo-positivist principle of the equivalence of meaning and verification have such a decisive role in quantum physics?

XIX

If the ratio between velocity and position is determined, and it is a reality that is in itself unknowable, then it necessarily determines

the subsequent state of a particle. That is to say, the subsequent
state of a particle is subjected to an epistemic law that is unknown
– one in relation to which the probabilistic law, which establishes
the connection between subsequent states, would inevitably be
inadequate. In so doing, however, one assumes as the foundation
of every scientific lawfulness the way in which events appear *in
the experience of becoming*, and, therefore, the way in which
micro-phenomena, *qua* events, appear as experienced in their
succession (namely, in a reading of a measuring apparatus or in
an observation of films and photographic plates). If, then, the
primary lawfulness to which the subsequent state of a particle is
subjected is nothing but the way in which that state appears in
becoming – namely, as a beginning to exist by becoming
something out of nothing – then, the determinate ratio between
velocity and position cannot be an unknown law. For such a law,
in pre-determining the subsequent state, would not allow one to
conceive of it as something that begins to exist by emerging from
its own nothingness. That is to say that the positing of that
determinate ratio must be a meaningless expression; and,
therefore, that that ratio – regarded, precisely, as the content of a
meaningless expression – has no reality: namely, it is a
nothingness. Precisely because this ratio is a nothingness, the
subsequent state of a particle – or, more generally, of an isolated
physical system – can be a beginning to exist that arises from
nothingness. And it is precisely for this reason that the
probabilistic laws that statistically predict this existence do not
constitute an inadequate description; on the contrary, they
adequately express every regularity that can be ascribed to events

that issue from nothingness: namely, the regularity described by statistical observations – the regularity of the taking place of chance as described by the laws of chance.

The subsequent state of a particle is an event that issues from nothingness not in the sense that the particle itself issues from nothingness, but rather in the sense that, in the preceding state of the particle, the determinate ratio between velocity and position of the particle is a nothingness. That is to say, the determinate ratio – which would have made the originary nothingness of the subsequent state predictable by anticipating it, and, thereby, entifying it – is a nothingness. It is from this being-nothing [*nientità*] of its own predictability, and of the possibility of being anticipated and entified, that the subsequent state ensues: it therefore arises from its own being-nothing. It is precisely because the subsequent state arises from nothingness that the probabilistic predictions of the subsequent state of a physical system do not express a limit of knowledge, but the essential limit that belongs to every thing insofar as it is a thing of the West: namely, its beginning to be out of nothingness.

XX

Reichenbach has attempted to demonstrate the indeterminacy of the position of a particle when its momentum is determined – and the indeterminacy of the momentum when the position is determined – by substituting the two-valued logic with a three-valued logic that would reject the principle of the excluded third:

that is to say, a logic that would posit, besides an existing state and a non-existing one, also a state that is neither existing nor non-existing, but, precisely, 'indeterminate'.

However, this attempt (towards which, in a way, Schrödinger's perspective also converges) is only an intermediate stage in the process through which the destruction of determinism is accomplished in quantum physics. Indeed, the indeterminacy of the position (or velocity) represents a contradiction: for what is indeterminate is not an existing being; but, at the same time, lest it be a nothingness, it must exist. Stating, therefore, that the position, or velocity, of a particle is 'indeterminate' means stating that a contradiction exists. Science, to the extent that it does not intend to submit to this consequence, must not therefore state that a particle has an 'indeterminate' position or velocity, but, rather, that it is contradictory to attribute a determinate position to a particle that has a determinate velocity. That is to say, it must state that, precisely because a particle with a determinate position and velocity represents a contradictory notion, the content of this notion does not exist: it is nothing.

It is true that Heisenberg and Bohr do not refer to a contradictory notion, but rather, by means of a neo-positivist language, to a meaningless statement. Except that, in its essential meaning, the neo-positivist concept of meaninglessness is precisely the concept of nothingness: the meaning of nothingness is present even when one believes one has nothing to do with the decisive categories of Greek ontology.

The Will to Power as Interpretation

XXI

The *epistéme* is the law that renders the occurrence of chance impossible: as such, it remains an impotent domination of becoming. With modern science, the will to power reaches the most radical form of domination precisely because it exposes itself to chance: namely, it destroys the immutables that make chance unthinkable. It also destroys – as has been mentioned – that immutable constituted by experience itself, insofar as this is regarded as an absolute datum that is isolated from any social practice. The world, insofar as it is dominated by science, is an intersubjective world. The critical self-awareness of the scientific practice, however, is not yet able to realise that the inclusion of the datum in the context of an intersubjective consensus, or lack thereof – the inclusion by means of which the datum obtains a scientific value – is an *interpretation*. An interpretation is a *will* that the datum have a certain meaning. More precisely, it is the will that the datum have a *further* meaning: namely, a meaning that is *additional* with respect to the meaning in which the datum consists. This additional meaning constitutes the content of the interpretation, and it is in relation to this content that the datum is constituted as an interpreted datum. The additional meaning is also a datum, albeit in a different way compared to the datum to which it is added.

An interpretation is a *will* because, in spite of the fact that both the interpreted datum and the content of the interpretation are data, the statement that the datum has an additional meaning does not, however, express a given connection – and neither does it express a logical connection of an analytic character. The existence of a connection is a problem – namely, it is itself given, but it is given as a problem (the problem is given [*è dato il problema*]): an interpretation is the practical resolution of a problem, in the sense that, precisely, it is the will that that connection exist. The bright spot that can be seen through the lens of a telescope already has, as such, a meaning; it has the meaning of being a bright spot. That the bright spot should be the visible aspect of a star, however, is an interpretation: namely, it is not something given or analytically established, but it is something willed. The bright spot and the property of being the visible aspect of a star are, albeit in different ways, data. That the bright spot should be the visible aspect of a star, however, is not a datum, but an interpretation: an interpreting will that, precisely, attributes to the bright spot the additional meaning of being the visible aspect of a star.

All data of experience are interpreted. It is *decided* – namely, it is *willed* – that a bright spot should be the visible aspect of a star. In the same way, it is decided that certain very complex events should be the social conduct of other human beings: *it is decided*, rather than ascertained or analytically established, that certain data should represent society; and, therefore, *it is decided* that certain data should represent an intersubjective practice that exhibits a consensus, or lack of one, as to what is understood as being 'given to me'. This decision is, precisely, the interpretation that wills that certain data have, besides the meaning that belongs to them, an additional meaning established by their inclusion in an intersubjective world. The interpretation *wills* that the datum be a social datum. For everything that is given [*dato*] is put in relation with those specific data that are interpreted as representing the social conduct. It is according to this relation that the intersubjective world of science is constituted. (And since the notion of 'given to me' is linked to the notion of the 'other', or of the multiplicity of the 'others', from which I can distinguish myself, it becomes apparent how the interpreting will, with the same gesture with which it wills the existence of society, also wills 'my' existence; and it therefore wills that the datum be 'given to me' [*il dato sia 'dato a me'*].)

Among the data that are interpreted as representing the social consensus, or lack thereof, the series of data that constitutes human language has acquired a primary function in the scientific activity. That there exists someone else's language, or that my interlocutors speak 'my own' language, is not a datum, but a decision. And even if, at a certain point, it has become a habit and a social constraint, it remains a decision – namely, the decision to assign to certain events (that is, to those events that we call the others' linguistic conduct) that additional meaning that consists in their being symbols of a meaning.

XXII

Therefore, if the data that confirm or falsify a prediction have a scientific value only insofar as there exists a social consensus concerning their existence and structure – and if the existence of a society and of a social consensus is something willed by the interpreting will – it follows that the existence of a confirmation of the prediction is itself something willed by the interpreting will.

Science dominates the earth because its predictions are confirmed and their confirmations enjoy the highest degree of social consensus: this not only means that the will to power – wherein science consists – is a will that wills domination, but that it is a will that establishes in what this domination is to consist. This is the case precisely because it is the interpreting will that wills the existence of a social consensus concerning the datum, which is an indispensable condition in order for the datum to be regarded as the confirmation of a scientific prediction – that is, in order for this very prediction to be successful. The success and domination of science are something *willed*: not only in the apparent sense that domination is the end that science aims to realise, but in the extremely more radical and elusive sense that the realisation of an end is not the production of a datum – for it is the will to power itself that decides that the datum that has been produced should be the realisation of the ends that science posits for itself. Which is to say, it is the will to power itself that decides that what exists today on earth is science's domination. The measure, or the criterion, with respect to which it is established that science dominates the world is not something external to science itself – something to which science should conform as to an absolute or an immutable; it is rather the very will to power of science that decides what the measure, or the criterion, must be with respect to which it is established that science itself dominates the world.

The will to power constitutes a domination because it constitutes a capacity for realising its own ends. This means that the will to power, insofar as it is embodied by science, is the capacity for exploiting the becoming of the world as a means for the realisation of its own ends; and it is this capacity because it does not dissolve becoming in the dream of the immutables, but it is a hypothetical prediction that sets itself up according to the logic of probability, rather than the logic of the *epistéme*. And neither does the will to power dissolve becoming nor, in addition, does it posit itself as a force antithetical to the occurrence of becoming: the will to power is the event that dominates every event, the occurrence that dominates every occurrence, the chance that dominates every chance.

The will to power, however, is not simply a capacity for realising its own ends: the will to power is first of all the will that decides that the taking place of the world is the achievement of its own ends; that is to say, it is the will that decides what the criterion should be according to which it is established that what takes place is science's domination. This decision, however, which interprets the taking place of the world as science's domination, is not an impotent wish or a new form of dreaming, precisely because it is within this decision that the world takes place in a form that can be interpreted – and, therefore, willed – as science's domination. This decision does not have any guarantee or any foundation, but it is within this radical lack of foundation that the operations of science occur alongside that very form of taking place of the world that the will to power decides to regard precisely as science's success and domination. It is in this way that, through modern science, the will to power dominates becoming.

XXIII

At this point, however, should we cast aside the suspicion that the originary form of the will to power is precisely that of the will for the becoming of the world to exist – the will for what is to be dominated to exist?

Indeed, things can be dominated precisely insofar as they are not definitively bound either to being or to nothingness, but rather oscillate between the two: that is, they become. For quite some time, my writings have attempted to show that the originary form of the will to power – and, concurrently, the originary form of the interpreting will – is that of faith; which is to say, the will for the becoming of the world to exist. The history of the West – namely, the history of the will to power – unfolds within this abyssal alienation, which is the very essence of every alienation, altogether hidden from the consciousness that Western civilisation has of itself.

The essence of this alienation has nothing to share with all the forms of alienation decried by Western thought – such as the separation from god, from nature, from moral conscience, from the ownership of the means of production, from psychic normality, from the ultimate truth of the *epistéme* – for all these condemnations are completely immersed in the essence of this alienation. For quite some time, my writings have attempted to show that the essence of this alienation lies in the belief – and, concurrently, in the will – that the things of the earth, insofar as they are things, are nothing. This belief is the hidden meaning of the will to power, which not only constitutes what posits itself as power, but also all the forms of refutation of the will to power that have appeared in the history of the West. The will that things be nothing is the essential alienation: namely, the essential unconscious of the West. It manifests itself as the will for the becoming of the world to exist, and it grounds the will to dominate the world by invoking god, the revolutionary praxis or scientific technics – that is to say, by invoking the immutables as well as their refutations. The thinking that catches a glimpse of the essence of this alienation dwells, therefore, in a different dimension compared to that in which the history of the West unfolds. It is set on indicating the structure of the two dimensions, as well as the meaning of their difference. It does not prescribe in any way what ought to be, but catches a glimpse of the inevitable course that the world truly traverses – beneath the 'Paths of Night', along which the will to power believes to be moving the world.

Part Two

Notes on the Problem of Intersubjectivity in R. Carnap's *The Logical Structure of the World*

1

The Unity of Knowledge

Positivism resumes and develops the Hegelian project of a unitary systematisation of knowledge. That is to say, an undertaking once again appears that in the history of Western thought has been pursued throughout the trajectory that unfolds from Aristotle to the scholastic *Summae*, and from Descartes to the *Encyclopédie* of the Enlightenment. The positivist unification of knowledge presents, however, a decisive novelty: in the previous systematisations, the unifying and subordinating principle is constituted by a philosophical-metaphysical-theological horizon, whereas, in this case, it is constituted by a *scientific* one. Concurrently, this latter horizon posits itself as the highest standpoint of reason, and therefore as the criterion according to which the value of every human conduct is to be established. In other words: if reality has a meaning that is accessible to humans, this meaning is to emerge from the ground of science, in such a way that the unitary systematisation of knowledge will have to be pursued according to the standpoint of science. The admiration for the natural and metamathematical sciences, as well as the intolerance for metaphysics and speculative philosophy, undoubtedly lies at the foundation of both the old and new positivist perspectives. However, they almost invariably originate from – that is to say: they are conditioned, and in a certain sense justified, by – an observation repeatedly remarked on and taken advantage of throughout the history of philosophy (one can for instance think of Descartes and Kant). This observation concerns the agreement among scientific researchers and the disagreement among philosophers – the existence, in each science, of a single body of doctrine, and the existence, in the domain of philosophy, of a plurality of mutually antithetical systems. The intersubjective agreement tends in this way to become the ultimate criterion (or at least an essential part of it) on the basis of which the rational value *of the content* of the agreement is established. Within neo-positivism, the repudiation of metaphysics is accomplished by linking this criterion to the method of verification. Within the internal development of this philosophy, however, an awareness arises as to the metaphysical character of the method of verification itself – and more 'liberal' formulations of this method come to be advanced – while continuing to retain the demands of intersubjectivity. Intersubjectivity comes in this way to be fully accountable for the rejection of metaphysics: it is a fact (or, at least, it is regarded as one) that humans agree with each other as long as they remain within the confines of accounts that concern the objects of experience, or certain aspects of it – and that this agreement disappears when they overstep that limit and construct statements concerning alleged meta-empirical objects. It is also believed that it is possible to provide a justification for this: there is an agreement with regard to empirical objects because they can be accessed and observed by everyone, whereas a privileged condition is required in order to grasp metaphysical contents. As a result, there can be no shared agreement between those who are privileged and those who are not; and even among those who are privileged, everyone is convinced of being more privileged than the others. Once again, as already for Kant, a reference to experience is an essential condition of intersubjectivity.

The 'fact' (or the 'attestation') of a disagreement among philosophers has been taken advantage of in different directions from those of neo-positivism (and of those several philosophical positions that today, in turn, resume the Kantian theme of metaphysics *qua* endless battlefield). It is the very claim of counting as a 'fact' and an 'attestation' that, of this fact or attestation, is to be put into question.[1] Within the philosophical thinking that still intends to save the demands of the *epistéme*, however, the content of that fact has been differently interpreted: in such a way that the disagreement among philosophers, as well as the plurality of antithetical doctrines, should rather come to appear as a systematic complementarity – according to what, for instance, Hegel has claimed – or as an antinomicity that is essential to the meaning and philosophical interpretation of reality. These are, however, precisely the paths from which every form of neo-positivist philosophy has distanced itself. According to this philosophy, therefore, the unitary systematisation of human knowledge cannot but signify the unification of intersubjective knowledge: that is to say, the unification both of those areas of knowledge in which an agreement among specialised researchers already exists – or its achievement can be predicted – as well as, more generally, of those areas of language in which there exists an agreement among the totality, or near totality, of speakers. If the project of a unitary systematisation of knowledge is already explicitly present in eighteenth-century positivism, the need to understand knowledge *qua* intersubjective knowledge becomes fully explicit with neo-positivism. This takes place, first of all, as a result of the particular attention devoted by neo-positivism to *language*, insofar as this is regarded as the natural medium – and, in fact, as the essential matter – of intersubjective knowledge.

2

Experience and the Intersubjectivity of Knowledge

The identification of the rational-theoretical order with the domain of the natural and mathematical sciences – and, therefore, with the domain of empirical-intersubjective knowledge – as well as the resulting anti-metaphysical stance constitute the fundamental determinations of neo-positivist *philosophy*. The project of a unitary systematisation of intersubjective knowledge constitutes instead the fundamental determination of neo-positivist *methodology*. This methodology, however, is a function of that philosophy. Within neo-positivism, they both constitute – under the guise of a 'neutrality' and of a disinterested 'rigour' – one of the most radical expressions of the will to power. The most serious shortcomings of neo-positivism are determined by the persistence in its philosophy of that epistemic stance that constitutes an inadequate form of domination of the world – as compared to the adequate forms constituted by science and by the scientific-technological organisation of existence. The original contributions of neo-positivism are, however, of a methodological character, and they concern first of all a 'correct' use of language. (The 'verification principle', for instance, is a form of persistence of the *epistéme* within neo-positivist philosophy.) It is possible to give this generic remark a more precise direction by noting that intersubjective knowledge is, in a rigorous sense, equivalent to language – namely, to sequences of signs and sounds. As a result, within neo-positivism, the ultimate reason underlying the attention granted to linguistic problems is precisely the (aforementioned) need for a unitary systematisation of intersubjective knowledge. A coherent use of the concept of experience (which, on the one hand, distinguishes the new positivism from the old, while on the other hand draws the former closer to the fundamental positions of phenomenology) must indeed raise to the rank of principle the fact that no plurality of subjects is given in experience, and that, therefore, what makes the *other* my kin – that is, a person – is not an empirical object (namely, the object of an immediate attestation). Others are given in experience *only* in the form of a behaviour (bodies, bodily movements, gestures, expressions, etc.), the most prominent aspect of which is a linguistic conduct. The reduction of others to their empirical behaviour conforms with the philosophical stance of neo-positivism, which, on the basis of the assertion of the meaninglessness of any meta-empirical

statement, recognises early on the meta-empirical character –
and, therefore, the meaninglessness – of the positing of other
subjects. The dogmatism of this stance, however, does not
compromise the value, from a phenomenological standpoint, of
the identification of the others with their empirical behaviour –
that is, the validity of the exclusion of a plurality of subjects from
the domain of experience.

From a phenomenological standpoint, or from the standpoint
of the logic of experience, the fact remains that intersubjective
knowledge cannot signify anything but a determinate relation
among linguistic conducts given in experience. Reducing the
issue to its simplest formulation: stating that there exists an
agreement among humans means that in comparable
circumstances they behave in comparable ways; and stating that
there exists an intersubjective knowledge means that in
analogous circumstances there exists an analogy between
linguistic conducts. Naturally, difficulties arise precisely at this
point, for rules must be established according to which these
analogies – and, therefore, their limits – can be identified. In
particular, the problem of the structure of language is to be
confronted. If the dogmatism of the verification principle is a
residue of the epistemic stance in neo-positivist philosophy, the
construction of intersubjective knowledge is first of all a scientific
problem. For the sciences aim to posit themselves, precisely,
as the sets of assertions that, according to a procedure to be
determined, enjoy the consensus of the totality or near totality of
linguistic conducts. That is to say, they either enjoy this consensus
if a certain psychological and cultural level has been reached or

they enjoy the consensus of a qualified minority (that of 'scientists'). This minority is then able, on the basis of those assertions, to predict and determine the transformations of the natural and social world that produce uniform reactions in the totality or near totality of behaviours (and, therefore, also of linguistic conducts).

The project of constructing a system of statements coordinated to uniform linguistic reactions (which is precisely the project of a rigorous construction of scientific knowledge) ends up becoming, in neo-positivism, a radical identification of the order of rationality with that system. At first, however, the emphasis is placed on the reference of language to empirical experiences: this reference is seen as a necessary condition – and, in fact, as the foundation – of the intersubjective linguistic edifice, as well as of its meaningfulness. In this framework, the sign system of the intersubjective language that constitutes science cannot therefore simply be identified with the rational order – precisely because it is founded on an extralinguistic empirical experience. However, the notion of experience attained in this first empiricist phase of neo-positivism presents a singular ambivalence, which constitutes one of the principal reasons for the move towards a rigorous identification of theoretical order and intersubjective language.

On the one hand, it is made sufficient clear that 'my I' does not represent the form that contains empirical experiences: Wittgenstein's solipsism aims, precisely, to rule out empirical subjects *qua* forms of experience, as well as to remark both that experience does not contain a plurality of subjects and that 'my I' itself is an empirical content among others. Concerning this point, neo-positivism comes to be in harmony with ample divisions of contemporary philosophy. Linguistic and contextual differences aside, idealism, phenomenology and existentialism all share this fundamental theorem. For instance, the transcendental I constitutes, within idealism (and first of all within actual [*attualistico*] idealism) a pure form of experience that is not to be confused with the particular subjects that belong to the content of experience. This is the case despite the fact that neo-positivists have never recognised the authentic meaning of the transcendental I of idealism, despite the fact that idealists have, in turn, regarded neo-positivism as a mere naive realism, and also despite the fact that, in the neo-positivist concept of experience, the figure of the *unity* of experience, upon which idealism has insisted, remains nearly altogether in the background, whereas a *plurality* of differences and experiences come to the fore. In any case, in the same way in which solipsism, when coherently developed, constitutes for Wittgenstein a pure realism, idealism posits itself, at the end of its process of internal absolution, as an absolute realism.

On the other hand, during this first empiricist phase of neo-positivism, the conviction is retained that the experience that gives meaning to the statements of intersubjective knowledge is *my* experience. In order to be meaningful, this theorem must presuppose the meaningfulness of the concept of experiences that are distinguished from the present one. A thorough application of the method of verification of a statement (according to which only those statements are meaningful that refer to a possible experience – which is, precisely, my experience) should instead lead to the acknowledgement of the meaninglessness of that concept, as well as to the consequent acknowledgment of the meaninglessness of the assertion that states that experience is my experience.

The focus here is not as much on taking note of this contradiction, as it is instead on remarking that the philosophical stance, which posits the 'being-mine' ['*l'esser mia*'] of experience as an absolute, comes to hinder the systematic stance of developing techniques for the construction of intersubjective knowledge. If, indeed, the source of meaning and value of science is my experience – if the edifice of knowledge is to be traced back to my observations – then, the final and decisive determinations relative to that meaning and value must be found, in the last instance, in a domain that is prior to that of intersubjective knowledge. That is to say, this domain is accessible only to me, and to no one else, and within it I could even claim to deny everyone else's knowledge – even if it were jointly and consistently advanced by everyone else – in case this were not confirmed by my experience. This conclusion can fully be comprehended from the standpoint of the control and epistemic anticipation of becoming; it constitutes, however, an obstacle to the project of highlighting and systematically unifying those linguistic conducts that can be interpreted as uniform reactions, and which, therefore, can be intersubjectively coordinated towards the ends of a scientific domination of becoming that the *epistéme* cannot realise (cf. Part I: 'Law and Chance').

In other words, if one intends to assume as valid those statements that are affirmed in the majority of linguistic conducts (or in a qualified minority), the divergence that should come to appear between the statements that express my experience and the statements that enjoy the support of the majority must be resolved by adjusting my linguistic conduct to that of the majority. This is particularly the case if the latter is able to transform the world in a way that I regard as being advantageous for myself.

3

The Protocol-Statement Debate

As a consequence of this assumption, it happens that, whereas in the initial empiricist phase of neo-positivism (Wittgenstein, Schlick) one still speaks of statements that have an *absolute* value (these are the statements that, in expressing immediate experience, are posited as the foundation of knowledge), in the revisionist phase (of which Neurath is the most convinced proponent) it comes instead to be denied that any statement should have an absolute value. And this is a legitimate consequence. Indeed, an intersubjective agreement exists among written or spoken statements – that is, among empirical and public events – and not among psychological processes that could only be controlled by the respective carriers. Among all statements, there undoubtedly exist those that indicate the immediate observations of various individuals; these statements ('protocol statements'), however, serve as foundation for all other scientific statements not by virtue of their absolute value, but rather because, *as a matter of fact*, they are the least likely to be modified or replaced. This *fact*, however, does not rule out the possibility of their modification or replacement, for there are no incontrovertible criteria according to which it would be possible to rule out the possibility that the compiler of the protocol was mistaken, suffered from hallucinations, attempted to deceive, etc. If, that is, the principle according to which the assertions that express an immediate content of experience have an absolute value (this is the principle of phenomenology) is one of the fundamental determinations of the *epistéme*, it is also to be acknowledged that when these assertions become an empirical fact (a visible sign or a sound), insofar as this empirical value is held firm, their referentiality and their very meaning become a problem. The construction of intersubjective knowledge consists, precisely, in considering statements *qua* empirical facts. It is therefore entirely consistent that, within this construction, every absolutism should come to be refuted. The ultimate origin of every anti-absolutism, as well as of every conventionalism of (revisionist) neo-positivism, lies precisely with the project of elaborating the system of intersubjectively coordinated signs that constitutes science.

From this standpoint, the so-called 'protocol-statement debate', which comes to involve all the principal exponents of neo-positivist thought, is the most important and concurrently the most ambivalent development of the history of this movement. The importance is due to the emergence of a predominance – *de facto* and *de jure* – of a methodological stance over the philosophical-epistemic one. The ambivalence is due to the fact that both opposing factions are convinced of sharing the same reference frame, when in fact they move within different ones: the empiricist faction (led by Schlick) lays emphasis on the 'philosophical' question that concerns the necessity of positing an extralinguistic ground of intersubjective knowledge; the physicalist faction (led by Neurath) lays emphasis on the methodological question concerning the necessity of eliminating any extralinguistic reference for the construction of intersubjective knowledge. What actually takes place, below the level of awareness of the protagonists, is that the process, which throughout the history of the West inevitably leads to the twilight of every absolute and immutable, comes to be mirrored in this debate – a debate that leads to the refutation of the absolute character of the statements that refer to present experience (the statements that Schlick calls *Beobachtungsaussagen* or *Beobachtungssätze*). If one takes into account that the original inspiring motive of the same initial phase of neo-positivism is constituted by the need to construct science as a form of intersubjective knowledge, the lingering of empiricist neo-positivism on a philosophical approach to the problem of intersubjectivity hinders and conceals that inspiring need. This need, however, is equally hindered and concealed by the physicalist attempt (which is, once again, a philosophical one) at identifying intersubjective language with the order of rationality. The very historicisation of experience assumes, within physicalism, both a 'philosophical' and a methodological significance. This significance is 'philosophical', insofar as this historicisation is due to the persistence of the idea that experience is 'mine', and that, as such, it cannot constitute the basis for an intersubjective agreement with others' experiences (whereby the existence of these experiences is presupposed); as a result, the agreement between my experience and that of the others can take place only on the basis of a linguistic conduct. This significance is methodological, insofar as the decision to bracket experience does not depend on a philosophical concept of the latter, but on the simple methodological intent to confine the enquiry to linguistic conducts. Moreover, physicalists remain on the methodological ground of a pure and simple analysis of this conduct when they remark that language is originarily intersubjective because even a statement that I have written must be interpreted in the same way in which a statement written by someone else is.[1]

4

The Presupposition of Intersubjectivity in The Logical Structure of the World

This complex interlacing of different stances appears in its entirety, with particular interest and significance, in the works of Carnap, who can be considered the main protagonist of the developments presented above. This is the case in particular for *The Logical Structure of the World*, 1928 (from here onwards: the *Structure*),[1] which has remained the most important 'philosophical' work of this prominent methodologist. The subsequent works certainly modify in many respects the analyses developed in the *Structure*, but they nevertheless come to join the horizon that is determined by that work – a horizon that Carnap has, in spite of everything, continued to retain. In other words, after the *Structure*, Carnap has not modified his general framework, but he has rather devised more radical and more rigorous solutions. In particular, he has successfully developed the methodological clues that are already present in his first work, while, however, invariably leaving in the background the philosophical framework that in the *Structure* competes against the methodological stance for the function of primary inspiring motive. In the Preface to the second edition (1961), this continuity of frameworks is explicitly acknowledged and maintained by Carnap himself. The general framework of the *Structure* is already present in the first pages, where Carnap states that the series of *Erlebnisse* – (lived) experiences – is different for each subject: '*Die Reihe der Erlebnisse ist für jedes Subjekt verschieden*' (§16).[2] The essence of this concept traces back to the beginning of Greek philosophy. Within sophistic epistemology, for instance, a prominent role is played by the principle according to which sense perceptions are different both for each person and in different times of the cognitive life of the same person. This principle is also retained by Plato and Aristotle, for whom knowledge is universal insofar as it is an act of the intellect, rather than one of the senses, in such a way that agreements among human beings take place on an intellectual level rather than on a sensory one. This implicit identification of universality and intersubjectivity can be considered a misunderstanding. For the plurality of subjects (and, therefore, the plurality of subjects that have different series of lived experiences) is not a datum of experience – and if it is not demonstrated it simply remains a presupposition – whereas the universal realises itself independently of the existence of a plurality of subjects that have a common intelligible content. (It will be seen later what becomes of intersubjective universality in Carnap's thought.) But through an implicit identification of universality and intersubjectivity, carried out since the beginning of Western thought, there appears, in its original form, the will that truth (the universal) should constitute an effective domination over all things – and that this truth should not, therefore, be exhausted by a private wisdom and concealed within the intimate dimension of a single person, but that it should enjoy everyone's consensus.

The essential remark to be made, which can be anticipated here (cf. paragraph 9 of the present essay), consists in noting that, in *The Logical Structure of the World*, the realist presupposition of a plurality of subjects, which have different sequences of lived experiences, grounds and determines a conceptual structure in which the notion of intersubjectivity is defined in a way that differs from the one that pre-determines that very structure. An oscillation of this kind can also be detected in Schlick's works. In '*Erleben, Erkennen, Metaphysik*' ['Experience, Cognition and Metaphysics'],[3] Schlick precisely distinguishes *Erleben* (immediate lived experience) from *Erkennen* (conceptual knowledge). Knowledge constitutes the domain of 'what can be communicated' ['*il comunicabile*'], because what can be communicated is what can be expressed by means of symbols, and knowledge consists precisely in tracing the object to be known back to other objects through which the original object can be known; this takes place by designating that first object by means of concepts that have already been coordinated with those other objects. This designation is *undoubtedly* regarded by Schlick as a symbolic relation or representation – and, therefore, as an element that can be communicated. What cannot be communicated [*l'incomunicabile*] is, on the other hand, the immediate content of experience (the *Erleben*), which is meaningful only for those who directly perceive it, and which no symbolism is therefore able to communicate to others.[4] It is clear that this distinction is meaningful only if, once again, the existence of a plurality of subjects is presupposed. These subjects, altogether differentiated with respect to the series of their *Erlebnisse*, can however communicate with each other symbolical and conceptual pieces of knowledge – which, therefore, unlike the *Erlebnisse*, belong to a public or shared dimension.

In the same page, however, this naively realist framework is contradicted by the remark that states that those problems for which there is no possible method of solution are meaningless; and the problem of the existence of other subjects is, for Schlick, precisely one of those problems. It should therefore follow from this remark that the same distinction between *Erleben* and *Erkennnen* is meaningless, for it entails precisely the positing of a plurality of subjects in the sense that has been indicated. Instead, nothing of the sort takes place, and Schlick continues to hold fast to this distinction, which remains one of the cornerstones of his thought. And it also remains one of the cornerstones of Carnap's *Structure*, which, essentially, is nothing but the systematic development of this distinction, and which repeats the characteristic misunderstanding consisting in the immediate identification of the definition of an object with its symbolic representation.

The misunderstanding is too exposed to be unwarranted. The reason consists in the fact that when neo-positivists talk about consciousness they *undoubtedly* mean an intersubjective consciousness. Schlick's argument *seemingly* aims to *demonstrate* that 'knowledge is what can be communicated *kat'exochén*' – namely, that it is intersubjective – whereas it in fact presupposes what it aims to prove. It presupposes this precisely because the designation of an object by means of concepts, which have already been coordinated with other objects, is *undoubtedly* regarded as a symbolic expression or representation of the object. This is precisely what takes place in intersubjective linguistic conducts in which 'I' render an object knowable 'to an other' by connecting the *name* of the object to other names that I assume are already known to my interlocutor. The question of knowledge is regarded from the outset as a question concerning intersubjective knowledge (and not only within neo-positivism, but also in broad areas of contemporary philosophical thought – which, in turn, inherits this, among other things, from a very distant past).

5

Intersubjective Knowledge qua *Structural Knowledge*

Section §13 of the *Structure*, which plays a crucial role in the entire unfolding of the work, is in this sense emblematic. It begins by stating that a scientific statement is meaningful only if 'the meaning of the object-names [*Gegenstandsnamen*] which it contains can be indicated [*angegeben*]'. The use of the verb 'to indicate' is to be emphasised here (a meaning needs to be 'indicated' only when one wishes to let others know what one is thinking), as well as, in particular, the fact that a statement is not considered with respect to its original intentional-manifestative value – which is indeed acknowledged in §164 of the *Structure* – but as a sequence of names: that is, of symbols.

The text continues by stating that this meaning can be indicated in two ways. According to the first one, called by

Carnap 'presentation', 'the object that is referred to is brought within the range of perception and is then indicated by an ostensive gesture'. It is clear that this can be asserted only when considering the dialogic relation in which, for instance, 'I' want to let my interlocutor know what I mean by a certain word. There is, however, a level that is prior to the dialogic one: this is precisely the level of 'referring to' and 'perceiving' the object, in which the actual intentionality of the reference has no need, in order to be meaningful, to bring the object within the range of perception and to indicate it by means of any gestures.

The second way of indicating the meaning of names is given, according to Carnap, by a 'characterisation': namely, by the unique definition of an object that indicates 'those characterising properties which unequivocally allow the recognition of the object that is referred to within the object domain under discussion'. Once again, the argument is undoubtedly formulated from an intersubjective standpoint (namely, thinking is immediately regarded as language insofar as it is an empirical event); which is, moreover, consistent with the project of 'indicating' the meaning of the names that appear in a statement. When an object is *present*, and insofar as it is *present*, there exists no possible misunderstanding that would let it be mistaken for other objects. The misunderstanding is possible either if the present object is included in preformed categorical domains – that is, if it is *interpreted* (and if it is interpreted through determinations that cannot presently be verified by experience) – or, and this is the relevant case here, if the object is not considered with regard to its presence, but rather with regard to its verbal designation (whereby it can happen that, while aiming to refer to a certain object, one speaks instead of a different one).

Intersubjective knowledge requires precisely the consideration of an object with regard to its verbal designation. If the existence of a plurality of subjects with different series of lived experiences is presupposed – and if it is presupposed that a linguistic conduct constitutes the domain shared by this plurality – it will then be possible to set out to construct a language in such a way as to eliminate every misunderstanding within communications, and in this way effectively guarantee the intersubjective value of scientific statements. The aim of *The Logical Structure of the World*, and more generally of physicalism, consists in nothing but this. The second part of §13 is particularly instructive in this regard. It presents the possibility of objecting that the definition of a name by means of other names requires, in the last instance, the presentation of an object. This claim, supported for instance by Schlick, expresses the (philosophical) need to ground language in experience. Nor does Carnap reject this argument: he simply brackets it, and states that 'within any object domain, a unique system of characterisations is in principle possible, even without the aid of presentations'. The reason for this historicisation of presentations (namely, of experience) – which is a methodological one, but which, at the same time, is determined by a certain philosophical conception of experience – is explicitly indicated right away: the possibility of leaving presentations out of account, in the specified sense, 'is the necessary presupposition of the possibility of any intersubjective and purely rational science'. This can be explained through the concept of experience that has already been noted, according to which everything that is concretely presented (*alles, was konkret aufgewiesen wird*) – that is, the lived experiences that constitute precisely the content of presentations – is something 'subjective'; namely, it is, as we know, 'the completely differentiated material' within every subject. The construction of an intersubjective science is then possible only insofar as no reference is made to the material, but only to the *form*, which, contrary to the material, can be translated into language. This last statement supposes an ontology according to which it is possible to distinguish object *properties* from object *relations*, and to distinguish the *structures* of relations from the relations themselves; and, therefore, to distinguish, respectively, 'property descriptions' from 'relation descriptions' and from 'structure descriptions' (§§10–12). In a relation description, the properties of the objects belonging to that relation remain unexpressed; in a structure description, the meaning of the content of the relation (and, therefore, all the more so the kind of objects that are in the relation) *also* remains unexpressed, and only the formal properties of the relation are indicated (the properties, that is, that constitute the object of that important area of logistics that is the theory of relations).[1] The structure of a relation is equivalent, as such, to the set of its formal properties, and it can therefore appropriately be expressed by means of a set of logistic symbols. 'Structure descriptions' form 'the highest level of formalisation and dematerialisation' of knowledge (§12). A system of structural statements is indeed completely identical to a system of 'characterisations' in which there appear no 'presentations': in both cases the reference to experience is, in the same way, left out of account.

The designation of an object through simple structural statements establishes a scheme of formal relations (that is, a structure) that is able to univocally indicate a single object: namely, which applies only to it and to no other object. This scheme is the set of formal relations that link this object, and no other, to other objects. If, within a certain object domain, two objects have the same structure, they cannot be distinguished within this domain; there remains, however, the possibility of considering other object domains, in which the formal relations that link the two objects are different. If, in spite of considering all domains of scientific objects, the two objects still preserve the same structure, then they are said to be different only 'subjectively', but not 'objectively' (§14).

6

Intersubjectivity and Objectivity

Science, *qua* system of structural statements, is therefore equivalent to the consideration of a pure 'objectivity', which is, at the same time, a pure intersubjectivity. Even if the – subjective – starting point of every knowledge lies with the contents of consciousness (*in den Erlebnisinhalten*) and with their mutual links, it is nevertheless possible to reach an intersubjective and objective world, which can be conceptually and precisely grasped as unique and identical by all subjects (§2). If, indeed, 'the *material* of the individual streams of experience [*der individuellen Erlebnisströme*] is completely different for each subject', on the other hand, 'certain *structural properties* are analogous for all streams of experience. If science is to be objective, then it must restrict itself to statements about such structural properties' (§66). The rationalist presupposition that intersubjective agreements should concern primary qualities, but not secondary ones (namely, quantitative aspects of reality, but not qualitative ones), becomes within neo-positivism the presupposition that these agreements should concern the pure formalisms of structures, but not the qualitative and concrete material of experience. This is essentially the same presupposition according to which logical forms should be preferred over primary qualities (which, from a rationalist standpoint, constitute the particular content of scientific knowledge), since mathematical logic has turned out to be able to develop the forms according to which *every* scientific discourse is realised. Consider the conviction that intersubjective agreements can be achieved only by restricting all statements to formal relations existing between things, without stating what these things are and, therefore, without attempting to describe them; this conviction applies what Whitehead and Russell had already accomplished in the domain of mathematics, by showing that every mathematical statement is a structural one, to the whole system of human sciences. The 'stream' – *die Strom* – of lived experiences remains at the basis of the structural system. The 'stream' is *the becoming* of the world. The structure – namely, what is 'objective' – has the task of making becoming intersubjective. The 'logical structure of the world' is, precisely, the system of the scientific anticipation of becoming.

The assertion according to which only formalised relations are 'intersubjectively transferrable' (§16) constitutes a presupposition that Carnap (among others) has never challenged – and one that he has continued to retain. This presupposition has remained at the basis of his whole subsequent scientific activity. (Challenging it would entail putting into question the notion that modern science is the most powerful form of anticipation and domination of becoming.) Carnap's subsequent syntactical investigations – and, in particular, *The Logical Syntax of Language* – do not represent a change of framework. On the contrary, within the perspective outlined by the *Structure*, they focus the attention on that logistic language, and on those formalisms, that in the *Structure* had already been regarded as constituting the content of intersubjective science. In other words, it is not the inadequacy of the philosophical framework of the *Structure* that is particularly apparent in the *Syntax*, as much as instead the inadequacy of the logistic conception (essentially inspired by Russell), which in that earlier work grounds the construction of intersubjective formalisms. Carnap's subsequent corrections to the *Structure* are, as can be noted in the Preface to the second edition, of a logico-methodological nature. Moreover, it is indicative that, in this Preface, a different way of accomplishing the task of the *Structure* is proposed – motivating this proposal by observing that this alternative way proceeds from a basis with respect to which 'there exists a greater degree of intersubjective agreement [*eine grössere intersubjektive Übereinstimmung besteht*]'.

It is of crucial importance, however, to note that if a structure constitutes the domain of objectivity-intersubjectivity, then science, *qua* unitary and complete system of structural statements, is to be conclusively distinguished from all formalisms such as those studied, for instance, by Hilbert for the axiomatisation of geometry. It is indeed to be asserted that the structural characterisation of an object is a kind of implicit definition. In an axiomatic system, however, implicit definitions are conventions that need only fulfil the requirement of not contradicting each other, and from which the statements concerning the object – or, rather, (according to Carnap) concerning the class of objects that is implicitly defined – can then be deduced in a purely analytic fashion. In a structural characterisation, on the other hand, a single empirical object is defined in such a way that not only is there to be no contradiction between the statements constituting the characterisation, but it is additionally required, as an 'empirical circumstance', that there should exist at least one object – and at most one – for which the formal relations expressed by that characterisation can be said to hold. This entails that what can *additionally* be asserted with regard to the object of the characterisation cannot entirely be deduced from the characterisation itself by means of analytic statements – but can rather also be given by synthetic statements (§15; Popper does not appear to have taken this into account in his critique of the *Structure*, in which all statements that can be expressed in the language of the characterisation should be 'all either analytically true or contradictory', cf. *Conjectures and Refutations*, London: Routledge, 2002, p. 355). This entails in particular that the characterisation itself is a synthetic procedure: precisely due to its consideration of the formal relations *of reality* (namely, of the 'stream' of the *Erlebnisse*). Knowledge is established as being intersubjective insofar as it is a pure formalism: a formalism, however, that constitutes the very objectivity of the real – the structure, precisely, according to which the real is realised.

As in the case of axiomatic structures, this does not prevent the constructional system from being able to be constructed at first as a pure formalism in which the relation to experience is indicated by a variable. By 'interpreting' this variable in a certain way, the constructional system is obtained, precisely, *qua* formulation of the formal structure *of* reality (cf. §121).

Carnap advances, in a neo-positivist context, a project that is akin to the one realised by Hegel in an idealist setting. Within the Hegelian *epistéme*, the structure is equivalent to the Idea *qua* pure objectivity and intersubjectivity, and the ultimate fabric of reality is expressed by a dialectical logic rather than by a mathematical one. In the same way in which Hegel distinguishes the dialectical method from the dialectical system, Carnap distinguishes *construction theory* (*Konstitutionstheorie*) from the *constructional system* (*Konstitutionssystem*). Both the dialectical method and construction theory consist of a methodological pre-conception of the possibility of the system. *However*, the dialectical system posits itself as the only possible systematisation of knowledge, whereas the constructional system is presented in the *Structure* not only as an outline, but rather as a *project* that explicitly admits, as a matter of principle, the possibility of other systematisations of intersubjective knowledge. In this admission, the methodological stance prevails over the epistemic one, and resolves – albeit under the sway of a presupposed philosophical conception of intersubjectivity – to develop the most adequate organon for the construction of scientific knowledge. In the *Structure*, Carnap repeats Wittgenstein's mistake, which consists in striving to develop *the* perfect language, while the 'principle of tolerance' only requires the indication of an operational language. Nevertheless, it is to be conceded – thereby confirming the active presence of a methodological stance – that, in the *Structure*, a kind of 'principle of tolerance' is already at work: one which, precisely, allows the admissibility of systematisations of intersubjective knowledge that differ from the one devised in that work. In the latter, however, Wittgenstein's mistake still persists, for in the *Structure* the possible systematisations of knowledge are not differentiated according to the employed logic, but only according to the different ordering of scientific objects. In the *Structure*, the process of emancipation from the *epistéme* does not yet reach the level of *The Logical Syntax of Language*. When, in 1931, Carnap further develops Neurath's proposal of assuming 'physical language *qua* universal language of science' ('Erkenntnis', II, pp. 432–465), he does not modify the framework of the *Structure*, but rather he simply takes into specific consideration one of the possible systematisations of knowledge that had already been envisaged in that work (cf. §59). The claim that physical language is the intersubjective language of science does not, therefore, contradict the *Structure*'s fundamental thesis, according to which an intersubjective scientific language is a system of purely structural statements: despite everything, this fundamental claim is retained – even though, precisely, different systematisations of structural statements come to be possible.

On the other hand, not only does this *sui generis* principle of tolerance render these different systematisations legitimate on the basis of a *single* type of logic, but, moreover, the systematisation outlined by Carnap in the *Structure* claims to stand as qualitatively different with respect to all other possible systematisations (and it is here once again possible to draw a correspondence with the Hegelian systematisation). It aims, indeed, to be constructed in conformity with the *cognitive order* of objects. In order to clarify the meaning of this concept (cf. paragraph 10), it is convenient to briefly outline the fundamental theses of construction theory.

7

The Concept of Construction

The term 'object' indicates 'anything about which a statement can be made' (§1). Therefore, each concept has 'its own object' – namely, object and concept are but two different linguistic ways of expressing the same content (§5). The 'systematisation' or 'systematicity' (that is to say, the 'system') of scientific knowledge consists, therefore, in a chain of definitions whereby all scientific objects are derived from certain basic objects – whereby, that is, all scientific concepts are traced back to concepts that immediately refer to empirical experience. This derivation-reduction, considered as to its specific technical characteristics, is called by Carnap the *construction* of an object. The constructional 'system' represents, as such, the ideal of positivist culture: for, within this 'system', it is concretely shown that the entirety of human knowledge can be reduced to experience – and that it consists, precisely, in a (more or less) complex processing of empirical experiences. More precisely (but still too indeterminately with respect to a rigorous definition), reducing an object x to an object y – or 'constructing' x from y – means transforming all statements concerning x into statements concerning y. The entirety of (scientific and rational) human knowledge is therefore translatable into statements concerning empirical experiences, and constitutes, as such, a single object domain. It is nevertheless necessary, within this single domain, to distinguish different object domains; the main specific object domains are the domains of 'psychological', 'physical' and 'cultural' objects.[1] The possibility of different systematisations of knowledge is given by the possibility of assuming the objects of each of these three domains as basic objects (where it is clear that 'cultural' objects are determinations of the social-cultural-historical world, and, therefore, are themselves determinations of experience), and, therefore, by the possibility of differently ordering the derived domains.

A specific notion of statement and proposition – which Carnap takes in particular from Frege and Russell – underlies this first set of considerations. On the basis of Frege's distinction between saturated and unsaturated signs (§27), a relatively independent meaning is granted to proper names (which are excluded, even if relatively, from the domain of *unsaturated* signs), and it is *presupposed* that, in a correct language, the subject of a proposition (which is the statement *qua* empirical sign) *must* be a proper name (a name, that is, that indicates a single empirical object). Language consists originarily of a speaking that concerns empirical objects, even if it can happen that unsaturated signs should come to be posited as subjects; these signs, however, do not refer to an actual and proper object (an individual empirical object), and it is therefore necessary to state that they refer to 'quasi-objects'. This inaccurate linguistic use, however, is allowed only if it is possible to transform the propositions having unsaturated signs as subjects into propositions having proper names as subjects.

By regarding propositions as simple sequences of signs, it is possible to obtain 'propositional functions' by removing from a proposition one or more object names – and to return to the original proposition by reintroducing them (§28). 'Permissible arguments' of a propositional function are those object names that, if introduced in an argument position, 'make sense' (§28): namely, they turn the function into a meaningful proposition, both in case the argument 'satisfies' the function (in which case the proposition thus obtained is true) and in case it does not (in which case the obtained proposition is false). Effectively, the notion of permissibility of an argument – which in Carnap's view (and more generally in the view of mathematical logicians) should indicate the circumstances under which the obtained proposition is meaningful – presupposes the very criterion of meaningfulness that should instead originate precisely from that notion. Stating that 'Berlin' and 'Paris' are permissible arguments for the propositional function '...is a city in Germany', whereas 'Moon' is not (§28), entails presupposing that there exists a single kind of false proposition. That is to say, it entails presupposing that the proposition: 'The Moon is a city in Germany' is 'a meaningless string of words' (whereas it is instead possible to rightfully assert that it is a false proposition, albeit not in the same way in which the proposition: 'Paris is a city in Germany' is false). Carnap, however, needs this notion of permissibility in order to define an 'object sphere' as the class of all objects that are permissible arguments for an argument position of a propositional function. Therefore, this class is a 'type', in Russell's sense of the term, but regarded as a class of real objects. Moreover, the acceptance of the notion of 'permissibility', which leads to the notion of 'object sphere', is prompted by the same reasons that have led Russell to the construction of 'type theory': namely, by the attempt to eliminate the 'paradox of classes'. (Cf. in this regard: E. Severino, *La struttura originaria*, Milan: Adelphi, 1981, Introduction, paragraph VI.)

Two propositional functions are coextensive if all the arguments that satisfy one of the two functions also satisfy the other one and vice-versa; the 'extension' of a propositional function is the quasi-object that indicates all the propositional functions that are coextensive with the function under consideration. The concept of 'construction' can now more precisely be defined by stating that an object x is constructed from an object y if every function that exclusively concerns x can be transformed into a coextensive propositional function that exclusively concerns y (§35). The role of this second function is not given by its being *this specific* function, but from its having the same extension as the first one (in such a way that any other coextensive function exclusively concerning y could play the same role). Because of this, it follows that every construction that leads to a new level of the constructional system is equivalent to the definition of an extension, and therefore either of a *class* (if the function concerning *y* has a single variable) or of a *relation* (if that function has multiple argument positions).

A class, insofar as it is an extension, is a quasi-object *relative to* its elements, and a relation is a quasi-object *relative to* binomials, trinomials, etc. of coextensive terms (which can also be called elements). Classes and relations, insofar as they are quasi-objects, belong to different spheres as compared to their elements – that is, as is also the case for Russell, they cannot serve as permissible arguments for propositional functions for which their own elements are permissible arguments: 'nothing can be asserted of a class that can be asserted of its elements' (§37). (If this were true, it would not even be possible to assert what Carnap nevertheless asserts: namely, that both classes and elements are objects; it would, in fact, not even be possible to account in any way for the relations that hold between these two kinds of objects.) The levels of a construction are object domains of different spheres such that each of them forms a domain of quasi-objects relative to the previous domain. Therefore, a constructional system is a system of quasi-objects that are such relative to the preceding level, and, ultimately, relative to the basic objects. This entails that science itself is a system of quasi-objects.

Given that a construction is equivalent to the definition of an extension, all the statements of a constructional system are extensional – namely, they can be represented simply by means of an extension symbol. The *Structure*, alongside Wittgenstein, excludes the existence of intentional statements – in particular, by taking advantage of Frege's distinction between the 'sense' and the 'reference' of a sign (§44–45). If a sense is the subjective mode by means of which a reference – namely, that to which a sign refers – is represented, so-called intensional statements do not express the reference, but the sense of a sign: namely, the subjective representations that, as a matter of fact, occur alongside the positing of an objective content. As a result, the absence of these representations from a constructional system does not entail any restrictions for the determination of objective-intersubjective knowledge. (However, already in *The Logical Syntax of Language* – §67 – Carnap reduces, in agreement with the principle of tolerance, the significance of the thesis of extensionality. He does so by regarding it not as a necessary rule of language, as he does in the *Structure*, but as an assertion of the possibility of translating an intensional language into an extensional one – and, at the same time, as an acknowledgment of the possibility that certain kinds of intensional statements could appear, which differ from the known ones and that could not be translated into an extensional language. Nevertheless, Carnap continues to regard Frege's distinction between sense and reference as a valid one – a distinction, that is, that advances once again a realist-phenomenalist framework according to which a sense is a subjective representation of a real thing, or structure, as this is in and of itself. It is indeed clear that references, as well, are contents of consciousness, and that only dogmatically can they be regarded as existing beyond subjective representations.)

8

Realist Language Formulation of the Concept of Construction

In a rational reconstruction, which constitutes the constructional system itself, pre-constructional statements of scientific and ordinary knowledge preserve, precisely by virtue of the thesis of extensionality, their 'logical value', but not their 'cognitive' one. That is to say, it is the (equal) extension of coextensive functions that is considered in constructional transformations, rather than those elements (which all belong to the meaning of a function) by virtue of which two propositional functions differ. A construction is, therefore, a translation in which what is preserved is the reference (namely, what is objective-intersubjective) of the statements concerning the objects to be constructed, rather than the sense (namely, what is subjective), as in usual translations between languages.

On the other hand, the construction of an object *a* – namely, the transformation of the propositional functions concerning *a* into coextensive functions concerning *b* – indicates, in a 'realist language' (namely, in the language commonly used for science and everyday life), that *b* is a necessary and sufficient condition of *a* and that, *at the same time*, it constitutes that through which *a* is known; that is to say, it is an 'indicator' (*Kennzeichen*) of *a* (§§47–49). Strictly speaking, the construction of *a* from *b* simply indicates, in 'realist language', that *b* is a necessary and sufficient condition of *a* – *and, therefore, that so is a for b*, for their propositional functions are coextensive. But in order to *know* this fact, it is additionally required that *b* should be an indicator of *a* (without any interchange here). In *Pseudoproblems in Philosophy* (published, in the 1961 edition, in the same volume of the *Structure*), the concept of construction is only considered with regard to this transcription into realist language. However, a different terminology is used there: 'sufficient constituent' (*hinreichender Bestandteil*, *Pseudoproblems*, §2, *a*) corresponds to the 'necessary and sufficient condition' of the *Structure* (§47); a 'nucleus' (*Kern*, *Pseudoproblems*, §3, *a*) is that sufficient constituent that corresponds to the 'indicator' of the *Structure* (§49).

A language having a scientific value can be realised *only* if it is possible to identify the indicators of the objects under discussion (§48). The nature of this requirement is clearly epistemic, and, if thoroughly understood, is in fact equivalent to philosophy's own demand, insofar as this is regarded as the elimination of every presupposition – *within* a certain understanding of the becoming of the world. Carnap, however, distances himself also from this radical conception of epistemic knowledge: according to him, knowledge is always equivalent to scientific knowledge, which takes, *qua* indicators, determinations whose foundational value remains, from a philosophical standpoint, a problem (even when, according to science, this value is 'infallible and always present'). According to Carnap, and more generally to positivism, what is known about reality originates from science: philosophy is a constructional systematisation that does not act as a *critique* of scientific knowledge (and, more generally, of any form of knowledge), but rather as its *clarification* – or, better, self-clarification – and sees to the elucidation of the purely objective-intersubjective structure of this knowledge. As such, philosophy regards as valid those demonstrative procedures – first and foremost, the method of indicators – that, within the sciences of reality, determine the configuration of these very sciences.

If someone were to object that one thing is an object and another its indicator – whereby it would appear that constructional definitions are not able to define an object – according to Carnap, it is necessary to reply that the authentic definition of an object is given precisely by its construction: namely, by the translation of the statements that concern the object into statements that concern its indicators. If, for instance, one wishes to distinguish between the feelings of a person (call these F) and the empirical behaviour that expresses them (call this K), it is nevertheless necessary to remark that all statements concerning F must be able to be transformed into statements concerning K (otherwise the content of the former statements would not have a corresponding indicator, and, therefore, would not have a scientific value). If F and K satisfy the same propositional functions, then they are identical for what concerns their logical value. The subjective representations that accompany F and K are certainly different, but, precisely, this difference does not concern the objective-intersubjective reality or its projection onto the constructional system (§52).

Keeping with the example, the proposition: 'Mr. X is cross' (a statement concerning F) and the proposition: 'The facial features of Mr. X are such and such' (a statement concerning K) have the same logical content (if the first statement is to have a scientific value) – for if the first one had a different content, this would not have an indicator, and it would therefore be a 'metaphysical' content. A logical identity entails that *everything* that can rightfully be asserted concerning Mr. X's ill temper depends on what is known about his behaviour (that is to say, it depends on the empirical elements that allow one to assert that X is cross). But F is identical to K – and not insofar as K is K (for, insofar as F is F and K is K, F and K are different), but insofar as F and K satisfy the same propositional functions. F, however, insofar as it differs from K, is a representation that does not refer to experience. According to Schlick and Wittgenstein's method of verification, every statement concerning F (insofar as F differs from K) is meaningless; according to Carnap, it is meaningless only if one forgets that it is a statement that concerns a subjective representation (namely, a statement concerning a 'sense'), thereby regarding it as a statement concerning the objective-intersubjective structure of reality (namely, a statement concerning a 'reference'). The anti-metaphysical stance is, here, of a Kantian rather than a neo-positivist kind (for it is possible to state, with the necessary modifications, that the Kantian limits of experience are turned into the limits of the logical structure, and that, also for Kant, meta-empirical statements are not meaningless in themselves, but are to be rejected only if regarded as actual determinations of reality, rather than as merely subjective representations).

This question also appears in *Pseudoproblems*, but with certain variations with respect to the framework of the *Structure*. In *Pseudoproblems*, it is first of all remarked that the formulation of a statement always occurs together with other representations that exceed the content of the statement. Some of these representations express a fact (*Sachverhaltsvorstellungen*), whereas others only express an object (*Gegenstandsvorstellungen*). The meaning of this distinction is altogether analogous to that of the Aristotelian distinction between judgement (which is always either true or false) and notion (which is neither true nor false);[1] Carnap himself asserts that *Gegenstandsvorstellungen* 'are beyond truth and falsity' (*Pseudoproblems*, §8). Whereas representations of the first kind must be able to be verified, those of the second kind are 'theoretically irrelevant', precisely because they do not assert anything, and if they are regarded as statements (namely, if one sets out to defend them or refute them through demonstrations), there emerge pseudo-statements and pseudo-problems, as well as, more generally, meaningless sequences of signs. In *Pseudoproblems*, meaninglessness originates, therefore, from regarding a notion as a judgement, whereas the validity of a notion consists in firmly regarding it as a notion (namely, as a non-predicative semantic content). In the *Structure*, meaninglessness originates from regarding a certain kind of statement (a statement concerning a sense) as a statement of a certain other kind (one concerning a reference); the validity of a statement concerning a sense (or, more generally, of a statement concerning subjective representations) consists in firmly regarding it as a statement concerning a sense.

9

The Realist and Constructional Meaning of Intersubjectivity in the Structure

Carnap's analyses, considered thus far, lead to a specific definition of intersubjectivity, according to which physical objects are indicators of other individuals' psychological processes. From a phenomenological standpoint (the *Structure* explicitly acknowledges the 'connections' between construction theory and Husserl's conception of a '*mathesis*' of immediate experience; cf. §3, as well as §164 for the notion of 'intentionality'), it is certainly to be admitted that the 'others' can be identified with their behaviours. At the same time, however, that a behaviour should be the indicator of a psychological dimension that does not belong to experience remains a problem – even if this behaviour is regarded by laymen, as well as by science (psychology), as an indicator and phenomenal projection of non-empirical psychological processes. This takes place on the basis of a – (more or less) self-aware – analogical reasoning, which coordinates my behaviour and my psychological processes with those of other individuals. This coordination, however, remains a mere hypothesis; but according to Carnap – and, more generally, to neo-positivism – the demonstrative and inferential procedures of science and common sense constitute a datum of which philosophy is, as remarked, simply a clarification. In this case, the clarification consists – assuming that empirical behaviours are indicators of other individuals' consciousness – in specifying that the representation of another consciousness, as well as of all its processes, is a mere subjective representation that has no real referentiality: not in the sense that it is correct to affirm that the other's consciousness does not exist, but in that both the affirmation and the refutation of that consciousness are meaningless.

This is *not* the realist concept of intersubjectivity, but, rather – even if differently formulated – Wittgenstein and Schlick's neo-positivist one. It is not an argument advanced by presupposing a plurality of subjects, but by positing the meaninglessness of this presupposition (albeit preserving the presupposition of science and common sense according to which behaviours are indicators of psychological domains). What we wish to emphasise here is that this notion of intersubjectivity is developed *within* construction theory and *within* the constructional system (which translates the prescriptions of the former into a system of concepts). As we have already remarked, however, construction theory and the constructional system are constructed precisely according to the very realist concept of intersubjectivity that, within constructional language, is posited as meaningless. *On the ground of a realist presupposition, a language is constructed within which that very presupposition, as well as its negation, are posited as meaningless.*

In *Pseudoproblems*, this contradiction cannot be detected to the same extent because the argument is developed from the outset on the level of construction theory; at the same time, this work also preserves the framework of the *Structure*, to which explicit reference is made for a more detailed analysis of the theses of construction theory (§6). In the Preface to the second edition of the *Structure*, Carnap refers to a more radical approach of the *Pseudoproblems* relative to the *Structure* – an approach that, in that Preface, he claims to still maintain to that day, in spite of the adoption of a more liberal method of verification. It should be noted that this – more pronounced – radical character has nothing to do with a rescuing of the realist presuppositions of the *Structure*, but rather concerns constructional language itself, which in this work refuses a *scientific* meaning to philosophical claims, whereas in *Pseudoproblems* it refuses *any* meaning to these claims.

A specific presupposition grounds the dismissal of the possibility that statements concerning F (considered as paradigms for all statements of this kind) could have, insofar as they differ from statements concerning K (that is, not insofar as they are coextensive with them), a real intentionality – an intentionality that is, therefore, transcendent. This is the presupposition according to which the scientific character of language consists in referring to things that both satisfy the same propositional functions satisfied by empirical experiences, and that, insofar as they differ from the latter, are therefore nothing but projections or different ways of expressing these same experiences. This is, in fact, the presupposition of the absolute value of the thesis of extensionality. From *The Logical Syntax of Language* onward, Carnap has acknowledged that it is not necessary to extensionally reduce all statements to ones concerning immediate experience, and that it is possible, by means of postulates, to introduce new statements serving as primitive propositions – provided that from these statements it should be possible to deduce the propositions concerning immediate experience. It is therefore no longer a question of a complete verification – namely, of a 'construction' – of scientific statements, but rather of their 'confirmability'.

The presupposition of the absolute value of extensional languages based on empirical experiences comes therefore to disappear, together with the basis of the anti-metaphysical stance of the *Structure*. The notion of confirmability of a statement can also be adopted by metaphysical knowledge (or, rather, by a certain kind of metaphysical knowledge), according to which a world beyond is introduced in order to prevent the empirical world from being contradictory (this is the kind of theoretical stance that neo-positivism, as well as most of contemporary philosophy, continues to neglect). This has the added benefit, relative to 'scientific' procedures, that the introduction of a metaphysical concept is equivalent to its own absolute confirmation; which is to say that, after the introduction of a concept, there is no need to deduce any of its experimental consequences – precisely because this very introduction consists in showing the necessity of understanding the empirical world as constituting an experimental consequence of a world beyond. This is the case even if the world beyond does not satisfy the same propositional functions that are satisfied by the empirical world. The neo-positivist critique of metaphysics is, therefore, an important example of contemporary culture's inability to definitively overcome traditional culture by means of the conceptual apparatus that is available to the self-awareness of the West.

Nevertheless, the aim of the *Structure* is not (as Carnap observes in the Preface to the second edition) to add further support to the principle of reducibility of all concepts to immediate experience, but rather to concretely outline a reduction or construction of this kind. That is to say, the aim is, or is meant to be, of a methodological-systematic rather than of a philosophical nature: namely, to actually make the concrete system of empirical-intersubjective knowledge work after all the generic anti-metaphysical philosophical talk – even though the different philosophical layers that have guided the formation of the constructional system are to be noted, and even though Carnap later reverts once again to a philosophical stance that is predominantly anti-metaphysical.

This visibly transpires in his 1961 statement, according to which he still regards the uncompromising anti-metaphysical stance of the *Pseudoproblems* as valid (*Structure*, Preface to the second edition, p. xi). For what concerns the question of intersubjectivity, this statement relies precisely on the distinction between *Sachverhaltsvorstellung* (judgement) and *Gegenstandsvorstellung* (notion) that has been recalled at the end of the last paragraph. In this case, it is of no use to ease the method of verification by substituting 'construction' with 'confirmability', for it is not possible to deduce any consequences from a notion (namely, from a semantic non-apophantic content). After having determined that an empirical behaviour is a 'nucleus' (or an 'indicator', according to the terminology of the *Structure*) relative to the domain of other individuals' psychological domains (*Pseudoproblems*, §§4–6), Carnap remarks that a proposition such as, for instance, 'A is joyful' (call this *p*) 'expresses the same theoretical content' – namely, the same 'logical value' – as the proposition: 'A is smiling, they have bright eyes, etc.' (call this *q*) (*ibid.*, §11). *P* effectively 'expresses more than the corresponding physical statement' (namely, *q*), 'but this more does not consist of an additional theoretical content, but expresses only [...] object representations [*Gegenstandsvorstellungen*], that is, representations which do not stand for any fact, and hence which cannot form the content of a statement' (*ibid.*). When I state *p*, rather than *q*, I express, in addition to what I express in stating *q*, 'a representation of a feeling of joy; certainly, of a feeling of joy in one's own [that is, my own] psychological sense, since I cannot know any other' (*ibid.*). The elements that justify the specific thesis that Carnap wishes to hold with respect to other individuals' psychological domains are all here.

And they are rather weak, for, in thinking that A is happy, I do not simply juxtapose a representation of a feeling of joy to q, but I *refer* this representation to A, and this reference results in a statement; as a result, 'the more' that is contained in p relative to q is not a *Gegenstandsvorstellung*. It is true that I draw the representation of the feeling of joy from my psychological state, but it is also true that I coordinate this representation with the empirical behaviour of the other: and this coordination constitutes a judgement. This is what I happen to do as an empirical individual. From the phenomenological standpoint itself, the proposition p (regarded as having a transcendent intentionality) constitutes a problem. It constitutes a problem, rather than a contradiction, because the representation of the feeling of joy is, indeed, drawn from my psychological state, but possesses, like every other determination, a meaning that can be dissociated from its current instantiation: it is precisely insofar as this meaning is thus made available that it comes to be referred (albeit as a problem) to a domain of consciousness that does not belong to experience. For, otherwise (namely, disregarding this availability), referring my state of consciousness (which, therefore, would be referred *qua* mine) to someone else would certainly be primarily self-contradictory (rather than a problem).

10

The Constructional Order According to Cognitive Primacy

The meaning of the passage at the end of paragraph 6 can now be understood. It is sufficient, in order for a constructional system to exist, that the statements of the system be 'reducible' to basic objects: namely, that for each object there exist 'necessary and sufficient conditions'. The reduction selected by Carnap in the *Structure* is, however, that in which these conditions are *also* 'indicators' of the reduced objects: in such a way that the latter are progressively traced back to the objects through which they are known. An object is said to be 'cognitively primary' relative to another one ('cognitively secondary') if the latter can be known through the former (§54); the indicator of an object is, precisely, cognitively primary relative to the object of which it is an indicator. 'Cognitive primacy' (§54) is not to be confused with the 'cognitive value' (§50) that has been mentioned earlier (cf. paragraph 8): whereas the constructional systematisation selected by Carnap does not preserve the cognitive value – namely, the 'sense' – of the constructed statements, but only their logical value, it nevertheless orders them according to a relation of cognitive primacy. Let us clarify this through the example used in the previous paragraph. P is a necessary and sufficient condition of q, and vice-versa; q, however, is an indicator of p, but *not* vice-versa, for everything that can be known about the psychological domains of other individuals is based on the observation of their behaviour, which is therefore cognitively primary. The *Structure*, therefore, selects the constructional systematisation in which p (cognitively secondary) is reduced to q (cognitively primary) – that is, in which p is constructed from q. However, the cognitive value of p – namely, the psychological-subjective value, or 'sense', that forms 'the more' that one finds in p relative to q – is not preserved in this construction. In other words (that is, using the terminology later adopted by Carnap), the constructional system selected in the *Structure* is equivalent to a 'calculus', whose 'interpretation' yields back the actual relations of cognitive dependency that exist between objects. The attestation of these relations is not of an epistemic kind, but – as already mentioned – is assigned to the empirical sciences, or, alternatively, results from the cognitive-inferential procedures of everyday life.

It is now necessary to determine the relation of cognitive primacy that obtains between the principal types of objects: namely, between physical, psychological and cultural objects

(§§17–25; §§55 ff.). Given that cultural objects are historical-cultural-social formations (for instance, a State, a set of customs, a religion), these formations 'manifest themselves' in the psychological processes of their 'carriers' (namely, of those in which, for instance, a certain form of religion is present; §24), and are 'documented' by those physical objects, produced by men, in which a cultural life expresses and crystallises itself (*ibid.*). This entails that cultural objects can be reduced to their own manifestations and documentations. Since documentations are human elaborations of matter, they require psychological processes in order to be realised (§55): as a result, all cultural objects can be reduced to psychological ones (*ibid.*). This notion of reducibility is, however, reversible, hence also an inverse reduction from the psychological domain to the cultural one is possible – in the background of which a philosophy of a Hegelian kind is presumably at work: 'a theory that explains the entire world process dialectically as the emanation of a spirit' (§56). But since the constructional systematisation of the *Structure* aims to realise itself in conformity with the relations of cognitive primacy, and since psychological objects are indicators of cultural objects (for instance, everything that can be known about a certain religion is asserted on the basis of the configuration of the psychological processes found in the carriers of that religion), the adopted constructional axis is the one in which cultural objects are reduced to psychological ones. Lastly, physical and psychological objects are mutually reducible (§57), but physical objects are indicators relative to objects of other individuals' psychological domains, whereas the objects of my consciousness – that is, the objects belonging to the domain of my lived experiences – are indicators of physical objects. (This latter assertion is not to be regarded in a phenomenalist-metaphysical sense, almost as if my perceptions constituted the foundation of my knowledge of 'external' physical reality: this can certainly be the way in which scientific-ordinary consciousness operates, but the latter ends up being deprived in the constructional system of every transcendent intentionality – as has already been seen for the indicators of other individuals' psychological processes.) Therefore, the order of objects in the systematisation advanced in the *Structure* is – according to cognitive primacy: one's own psychological objects, physical objects, other people's psychological objects, cultural objects.

The efforts spent in the *Structure* to neutralise every metaphysical interference within scientific and ordinary knowledge (both of which provide the real content of this constructional ordering) are undoubtedly remarkable, and so are the precautions taken in order to distance the constructional system from both idealist and materialist metaphysical systems. Particularly interesting, in this respect, is the whole set of considerations aimed at clarifying how the reduction of cultural objects to psychological ones – as well as the reduction of other individuals' psychological objects to physical ones, and of the latter to one's own psychological objects – does not entail, for instance, that a religion *consists* of psychological processes (§56), or that someone else's consciousness *consists* of physical objects. What objects are 'in-themselves' is a question ('a problem of essence') that Carnap leaves to metaphysics (§161). The 'reduction' of an object to an another one only concerns the translatability of the statements concerning the two objects in question: namely, the possibility of speaking about one of the two in terms of the other one (once again, with the proviso that only the logical value of the first object be preserved, and not necessarily its sense). If, therefore, one wishes to speak of the 'essence' of an object, one is to refer to its 'constructional essence', which consists in the determinate way in which the object 'is embedded in the constructional context of the system', and, in particular, in the determinate way in which 'this object can be derived from basic objects' (§161). It has been shown how, in a constructional system, objects belong to different levels because they belong to different spheres – in such a way that the objects of a sphere cannot be regarded as permissible arguments for the propositional functions that concern the objects of a lower level. The autonomy of the different kinds of objects is in this way guaranteed – arguably, over-guaranteed. The possibility of constructing a system based in the physical domain – namely, a system in which cultural and psychological objects are reduced to physical ones (§§59, 62) – has therefore nothing to do with a materialist metaphysics according to which all objects are, in their essence, physical processes. Within construction theory, the (methodological) task of developing the apparatus of intersubjective communication is, however, determined in various ways by an epistemic stance: both in the sense that at the basis of the neutralising argument there is a non-neutralised stance, as well as in the sense that the neutralisation attempt is correlative with structures that are epistemic in nature, such as the one of cognitive primacy. The possibility of different constructional arrangements of objects is analogous to Max Weber's critique of the epistemic attempts that aim to establish irreversible connections between phenomena and their causes (as it happens, for instance, in the Marxist principle according to which the economic structure is, 'in the last instance', the determining factor). The theory of cognitive primacy, however, appears once again as an irreversible coordination of an epistemic kind.

With respect to the neutrality of experience, Carnap remarks: 'At the beginning of the system, lived experiences must simply be taken as they are given; the claims of reality or non-reality that appear in connection with them [namely, the assertions that determine the content of experience as being real or non-real] will not be accepted; rather, these claims will be "bracketed" – namely, a phenomenological "suspension" (*epoché*), in Husserl's sense, will be exercised' (§64). The distinction between 'real' and 'non-real', 'I' and 'you', is, on the other hand, introduced only at a more advanced stage of the constructional system. 'Methodological solipsism', therefore, 'is not to be interpreted as if, to begin with, we wanted to separate the '*ipse*', or the 'I', from the other subjects, or as if one of the empirical subjects were being singled out and regarded as being the epistemological subject' (§65). Had Carnap, in the *Structure*, been rigorously faithful to this phenomenological-methodological framework of the argument, the whole meaning of the constructional system would have been lost. For it is precisely by virtue of the fact that the reality of a plurality of subjects is presupposed that, within the horizon of the *Structure*, the argument sets out to construct intersubjective knowledge referring to the structural properties of the material of the individual streams of experience, rather than to the material itself. The interference between the two standpoints – the phenomenological-methodological one and the realist one – can be verified in two surprisingly close points of the *Structure*: we are referring to §64 and §65 – in which experience is freed, with sufficient clarity, from any presuppositions of a realist or phenomenalist kind – as well as to §66, in which the realist presupposition of a plurality of subjects is explicitly asserted. Effectively, as has already been remarked, a realist conviction is at work at the origin of the *Structure*: one shaped by the awareness that experience is *my* experience, differentiated from the experience of others with respect to its content. The constructional system is developed within this subjectivist perspective (namely, it indeed takes place that 'one of the empirical subjects is singled out and regarded as being the epistemological subject'), and, in this development, a neutralised notion of experience is assumed as foundation of the system. In other words: remaining within my experience (this is the underlying subjectivist perspective), I construct the apparatus that I suppose will put me in communication with other experiences; and, within this construction, I make use of a non-subjectivist notion of experience (which, nevertheless, appears within a subjectivist conception of experience). Two different stages of the will to power express themselves through the interference between the realist-phenomenalist presupposition of a plurality of subjects and the neutralisation of experience: the stage at which the will to power wills the real existence of a specific consciousness – that of the carriers of the consensus without which that power itself would not exist – and the stage at which the will to power realises that not only are the calculations and computations of the consensus (and, therefore, of the effectiveness of power) not supported by the absolute positing of that real existence, but that they are actually hindered by it. In the *Structure*, this second stage unfolds within the first one, without yet succeeding in superseding it.

11

Elementary Lived Experiences and the Reason for their Unanalysability

Experience, assumed as foundation of the structural system, is constituted, on the one hand, by the stream of lived experiences (the basic elements of the system), and, on the other hand, by the basic relation(s) that obtain among lived experiences – namely, those relations to which all the further processing of experience is to be traced back. Concerning the first of these two aspects, it is certainly the case that the atomic constituents of experience – for instance, the simplest sensations or perceptions – are not assumed as foundation of the system; in this regard, the difference with respect to a systematisation of a Wittgensteinian kind is undoubtedly significant. However, it is also the case that, relative to the system, elementary lived experiences are assumed as indivisible units: and, therefore, once again as atomic constituents. Each lived experience is indeed equivalent to the entirety of experience at a certain moment in time, and the stream of lived experiences is the flowing stratification [*stratificazione fluente*] of sections respectively constituted by single elementary lived experiences. This stream is therefore equivalent to the unity-totality of time. This is the trait that differentiates the basis of the *Structure* from the basis of Wittgenstein's *Tractatus*, for each lived experience is the collection of all atomic and complex constituents of experience at a certain instant in time.

The adoption of this kind of basis is a *choice* (for, in the *Structure*, the possibility is acknowledged of systems with different bases, including therefore what Wittgenstein refers to as atomised bases). The rationale of that choice, however, still consists in an attempt to abide, within the constructional order, by the relation of cognitive primacy. Total collections are, as such, cognitively primary relative to their components. Since 'experience' – considered as the unity-totality of lived experiences (§67) – is the collection of all collections, it follows that experience is 'cognitively primary relative to everything else'. It is therefore cognitively primary relative to every particular or atomic content of experience itself, in the same way in which in *Gestaltpsychologie* a total impression is cognitively primary with respect to single sensations (*ibid.*). It is once again more interesting, however, to consider the relationship with the logic of idealist philosophy. The epistemic meaning of the Hegelian assertion, according to which 'the true is the whole', is projected – while being partly confirmed and partly transformed in a methodological-functional way – onto the assertion according to which total impressions are cognitively primary relative to single sensations (which, as such, are the result of an abstraction). An analogous projection can be detected between the principle of the *Structure* according to which the scientific meaning of objects is given by their reciprocal relations in the constructional system, and the Hegelian principle according to which knowledge does not presuppose its objects – the meaning of which, therefore, emerges as a result of the process that posits them.

In §68 of the *Structure*, the reason for assuming elementary lived experiences as 'unanalysable units' in the constructional system is presented in the following way. Since every level of the construction consists either in the formation of a class or in the formation of a relation, the first level of the system must be given either by classes or by relations between basic elements; the second level must be given by classes of classes and relations of the first level, as well as by relations among classes and among relations of the first level. It follows that a construction only constitutes a synthesis of elementary lived experiences, but not an analysis – and, therefore, that elementary lived experiences cannot be analysed through a constructional procedure. Any kind of treatment or consideration of the elementary units is then possible only by including them in an ordered system of relations. Indeed, the constructional arrangement of classes and relations forms that *structure* of experience that posits itself as the objective and – at the same time – intersubjective content of scientific knowledge, and which is, precisely, the ordered system of relations that contains elementary lived experiences. We are saying that the assertion according to which (in a constructional order) lived experiences appear only as unanalysable units is equivalent to the assertion according to which scientific knowledge is possible only to the extent that it disregards the material, and only expresses the *form* – which consists, precisely, in the network of relations surrounding each lived experience. (As a result, the concrete content of experience is not conveyed in that expression – and experience itself remains, therefore, an unanalysable unit.) This is the meaning that underlies §68, and which had distinctly been reiterated in §66 ('science is, per its own essence, science of structure, and, therefore, there is a way of constructing what is objective starting from the individual stream of lived experiences'). This is the case even though, in §68, the question of intersubjectivity is not explicitly formulated, and its formal aspect is instead emphasised – namely, the notion that the elements of a structure are, within that very structure, unanalysable units. As a consequence, in the specific case, the problem arises of constructing, on the basis of lived experiences, those particular sense qualities that are usually regarded as being the constituents of lived experiences. This is the problem of indicating the properties of the unanalysable elements.

It is then necessary to devise a constructional procedure that would not constitute an actual analysis, but rather a 'quasi-analysis': a way, that is, of talking about unanalysable units (and about anything that is unanalysable), which would allow the characterisation of these units without describing them. This would therefore constitute a synthetic procedure that is equivalent, precisely, to the structural characterisation of experience that has been discussed earlier, and which is now to be more concretely presented. We are indeed facing the concrete construction of the apparatus through which Carnap believes he can achieve the communication of objective-intersubjective knowledge.

12

The Method of Quasi-Analysis: Goodman's Critical Observations

A statement that concerns unanalysable units cannot constitute a property description, but only a relation description; since all the statements of the constructional system are extensional (and, therefore, so are all statements expressing fundamental relations between lived experiences), relation descriptions must be given in terms of link descriptions (where a link is, precisely, the extension of a relation). In this case, it is not the specific meaning of the relations between lived experiences that is considered, but only the extension of these relations, by enumerating (or indicating in any other way) the pairs of terms among which the basic relations (or relation) obtain (§69). While a quasi-analysis does not result in the indication of the actual constituents of a lived experience, it however indicates 'formal substitutes' of these constituents – it indicates, that is, quasi-ingredients – and is carried out according to a procedure that is thoroughly analogous to the procedure of proper analysis. As a result, §70, in which Carnap concretely illustrates this procedure, assumes a particular importance.

Before starting the discussion, it is necessary to warn once again that the whole argument is meaningful only if it is interpreted according to the principal axis of the *Structure*: namely, the one given by the question of intersubjectivity. If (on the basis of the conviction that there exists a plurality of subjects with completely different streams of lived experiences) I intend to let another person understand what I mean by the word 'red', I have to give up all qualitative descriptions (property descriptions), for, as a matter of principle, the possibility always exists that I could be talking about a different shade or colour, or even perception, as compared to the one discussed by my interlocutor. If, instead, I succeed in indicating all the relations (relation descriptions) that exist among red things, I will then obtain a *network* of relations, which is truly unlikely to have the same *pattern* that I would obtain by considering green things instead of red ones. I can then use the pattern of this network of relations, considered in its formal aspect (namely, adopting its structure), as a 'substitute' for those qualitative determinations that would never allow me to let my interlocutor understand what I mean by the word 'red'. I can use it, that is, as an intersubjective (and, at the same time, constructional) definition of 'red', in which I do not indicate the actual constituents of red, but only constituents that are *sui generis*. This is, very concisely, the perspective adopted by the *Structure* (which consists of presupposing that formalisms make communication and intersubjective agreements possible).

Let us consider an analytic procedure, and let us set forth the following problem: given a certain number of things, whose ingredients (or properties) are not known, the task is to infer these ingredients by means of a link description – that is, by indicating the list of pairs of terms for which a certain given relation holds. *Example*: a certain number of things is given, each of which has one or more colours out of a series of three colours.[1] Without knowing which colours each thing has, and knowing only for which pairs of things a relation of 'colour kinship' holds (that is, which pairs have at least one colour in common), the task is to define each of the three colours by determining their 'colour classes' – namely, the classes of things that have a colour in common (either together with other colours or not).

Each thing that has more than one colour belongs to multiple classes. There are therefore three partially overlapping classes. Each class satisfies the two following properties: (A) the elements of each pair of the class are 'colour-akin' – namely, each pair must be contained in the series of pairs that stand in a relation of colour kinship to one another; (B) colour classes are the largest possible classes that satisfy the property (A) – namely there can exist no thing (belonging to the group of things under consideration) that stands in a relation of colour kinship to all the elements of the class, while not belonging to the class itself. This second property may fail to hold if certain adverse conditions obtain, which will be addressed later on. Carnap names the classes constructed on the basis of properties (A) and

(B) 'similarity circles'. Let us indicate the three colours by the conventional symbols k_1, k_2, k_3 – for we do not know whether k_1 stands for green, red or blue. Let us say that if a thing is an element of k_1, its colour will be k_1, and if a thing has two colours, it will be an element of, say, k_1 and k_2. It is then possible to determine, for each of the considered things, 'which colour it has' (and which other things have the same colour) on the basis of the series of pairs that stand in a relation of colour kinship. That is to say, it is possible to indicate the constituents of each thing not in terms of concrete qualities, but rather in terms of classes that have certain things, and not others, as elements.

Concretely: let us suppose that six things are given, that each of them is indicated by a number, and that the letters r, b, g indicate the three colours (red, blue, green) that can be found in each thing (therefore, for instance, 1.br indicates that thing, out of the given six, that is partly blue and partly red); let us further suppose that the colours are distributed among the six things according to the following Table I:

Table I

1.br	4.g
2.b	5.r
3.bg	6.bgr

In an intersubjective communication, however, it is not possible to let someone understand what is meant by the words indicating the concrete qualities b, r, g. It is then necessary to verify whether it is possible to give a definition of the three colours relying only on a list of the pairs that stand in a relation of colour kinship (thereby indicating neither which colours a thing has nor which colours are shared by two things). On the basis of Table I, the list in question is presented in the following Table II:

Table II

1:1	2:2	3:3	4:4	5:5	6:6
1:2	2:3	3:4	4:6	5:6	
1:3	2:6	3:6			
1:5					
1:6					

It is therefore necessary to determine, on the basis of Table II alone, the colour classes relative to the six things. Since these classes are the classes in which the elements are all, and only, numbers that in Table I are followed by the same letter, the validity of this procedure is verified through a comparison with Table I. The classes thus obtained must satisfy the two properties (A) and (B) indicated above, for (A) and (B) uniquely characterise a class. Table II is constituted, precisely, by the list of pairs that – according to what is required by (A) – includes all pairs that can appear in the obtained colour classes, and that – according to what is required by (B) – includes none of the (six) things that, while not belonging to a class, would be paired in this Table with all the other elements of this class.

Now, by applying (A) and (B), let us list all the things that are paired with 1. We obtain the class [1 2 3 5 6]. This class, however, does not satisfy (A), for the pairs 2:5 and 3:5, in spite of being pairs of this class, are not listed in Table II. In order to obtain a colour class, we should then proceed either by eliminating 5 or by eliminating both 2 and 3. In the first case, we obtain the class [1 2 3 6], which satisfies both (A) and (B). Let us call this class k_1. In the second case, we obtain the class [1 5 6], which also satisfies both (A) and (B), and which we call k_2. A third colour class is obtained by listing all the things that are paired with 3. We obtain the sequence 1, 2, 3, 4, 6, in which, however, the pairs 1:4 and 2:4 are not listed in Table II: therefore, once again, we shall have to eliminate either 4 or both 1 and 2. Since, in the first case, we would obtain once again the class k_1, we are left with the second case, which leads to the class [3 4 6]: this class satisfies both (A) and (B), and we call it k_3. It can easily be shown that no other class exists that satisfies both (A) and (B). If we now compare the obtained classes with Table I, we note that k_1 [1 2 3 6] includes all, and only, blue things (*b*); that k_2 [1 5 6] includes all, and only, red things (*r*); and that k_3 [3 4 6] contains all, and only, green things (*g*). Therefore, the application of rules (A) and (B) to Table II allows one, by indicating the groups of objects that have a colour in common, to give a structural, rather than qualitative, definition of the three colours. At this point, it is certainly not possible to let my interlocutor concretely understand what I mean by the words 'blue', 'red', 'green'; but we shall nevertheless be able to understand each other regarding the formal or structural properties of these qualities – and, first of all, regarding the fundamental and distinguishing property by virtue of which a quality pertains to a certain group of things rather than to a different one.

The concrete example just presented does not appear in Carnap's text (which, however, gives all the necessary indications for its realisation), but rather in Chapter V of Nelson Goodman's essay, *The Structure of Appearance*, 1951, pp. 119 ff. This chapter, devoted to the *Structure*, contains that series of critical observations due to which Carnap has later deemed it necessary to provide a different basis for the constructional system. In §70, the possibility is briefly mentioned, in passing, that 'adverse circumstances' could appear, as a result of which property (B) would come to no longer hold: if one of the three colours (for instance, blue) is a 'companion' of another one (for instance, of red) – that is, it never appears without this other one – it is then impossible to construct the class of the colour blue; and, therefore, it is impossible to structurally define the colour blue. Were, indeed (cf. N. Goodman, *ibid.*, p. 122), the colours distributed as it appears in the following Table III, rather than according to Table I:

Table III

1.*br*	4.*g*
2.*b*	5.*bgr*
3.*bg*	

Then the list of pairs of things that stand in a relation of colour kinship would have been:

Table IV

1:1	2:2	3:3	4:4	5:5
1:2	2:3	3:4	4:5	
1:3	2:5	3:5		
1:5				

Proceeding as earlier, we obtain, by listing all things paired with 1, the class [1 2 3 5], which satisfies both (A) and (B), and which we call k_1. Comparing with Table III, we conclude that k_1 is the class of blue things. However, as can be inferred from Table III, the class [1 5] is also a colour class (namely, it is the class of things that, within the series of five things considered here, are red). Nevertheless, this class cannot be constructed on the basis of (A) and (B), since, in Table IV, 2 is paired with both 1 and 5, and must therefore be included in this class; and the same can be said about 3. As a result, on the basis of (A) and (B), it is not possible to keep the class [1 5] separate, and we end up, once again (that is, by having to include 2 and 3), with that same class [1 2 3 5], which should have instead been used to define the colour blue. It is not possible, in this case, to define the colour red separately from the colour blue: that is to say, the method of determination of intersubjective definitions cannot be applied.

Carnap holds that – unless there exist systematic connections in the colour distribution – the occurrence of adverse circumstances, which do not allow the functioning of that method, is all the more unlikely the larger the number of things considered and the smaller the average number of colours of each thing. Goodman observes that not only does there exist no method for determining whether, in a certain object sphere, an adverse circumstance will occur, but that, by applying the procedure under consideration to elementary lived experiences (which correspond, precisely, to the colours of the example), it is not the circumstance predicted by Carnap that occurs, but the opposite one. That is to say, the average number of qualities that pertain to the single elementary lived experiences in no way tends to decrease (*ibid.*, p. 123). What is more relevant, as Goodman correctly observes, is that the exclusion of systematic connections in the colour distribution (an exclusion that, according to Carnap, is supposed to guarantee that the occurrence of adverse circumstances remains unlikely) constitutes a *petitio principii*, for an adverse circumstance is precisely a kind of systematic connection (*ibid.*, pp. 123–124). Lastly, Goodman considers the case in which the situation indicated by the following Table V is given:

Table V

1.*bg*	3.*br*	5.*b*
2.*rg*	4.*r*	6.*g*

Evidently, the adverse circumstance does not occur here; nevertheless, the procedure of intersubjective definition fails to achieve its goal. Indeed, the list of pairs is in this case:

Table VI

1:1	2:2	3:4
1:2	2:3	3:5
1:3	2:4	4:4
1:5	2:6	5:5
1:6	3:3	6:6

According to Table V, things 1, 2, and 3 do not form a class; nevertheless, the sequence [1 2 3] satisfies both (A) (for all the things of this pseudo-class are listed in Table VI) as well as (B) (for no single thing, which does not belong to this pseudo-class, is paired in Table VI with all the terms of this pseudo-class). One should therefore state that [1 2 3] is a proper colour class; but upon checking which colour 1, 2 and 3 have in common, it is seen that they have none. This failure occurs in all cases in which things are distributed according to the following formula:

$$1.abc \qquad 2.bcd \qquad 3.cde \qquad 4.def^2$$

13

Scientific-Ordinary Knowledge and Constructional Systems

Given that the basis of a constructional system comprises, on the one hand, basic elements (in the *Structure*: elementary lived experiences), and, on the other hand, the basic relation(s) according to which elements are first posited – and given that lived experiences are cognitively primary relative to single perceptions and sensations – it follows that basic relations are, however, cognitively primary relative to lived experiences (§§7, 75). These relations constitute the '*a priori* form' (Carnap explicitly refers to neo-Kantianism, *ibid.*: cf. in addition §83), whereas lived experiences constitute the '*a posteriori* matter'. In the text, the serious difficulties that originate from assuming form as being cognitively primary relative to matter (an error against which Kant had already distinctly warned) are not even suspected. Once again, however, this theoretical deficiency can lucidly be explained by taking into account the interference played by the question of intersubjectivity, as a result of which the argument ends up referring, rather than to knowledge as such, to knowledge *qua* intersubjective communication. As we have, by now, repeatedly remarked, what is prior from the standpoint of communication is not the concrete material of experience, and neither is it its synthesis with the form that accompanies it: what is prior is pure form – the 'structure of experience'.

It is then necessary to select those relations (or that relation) that are able to express (logically, rather than psychologically) all the determinations that, according to science (and common sense), pertain to the world. Therefore, the criterion for the selection of the basic relation is given by the actual possibility of reducing all scientific objects – and, first of all, all physical objects – to the selected relation. Since, in the *Structure*, this reduction is only roughly sketched – and with important deficiencies – and since it is acknowledged that the *content* of the constructional system constitutes a kind of attempt (cf. §84), the whole argument concerning basic relations is equivalent to a working hypothesis (cf. §83) – to which Carnap will later prefer different ones, which appear to provide greater guarantees of success (cf. *Structure*, Preface to the second edition).

In the *Structure*, however, the 'recollection of similarity' (*Er*) is posited as the only basic relation. This is a specific kind of 'partial similarity' relation (*Ae*). Two lived experiences, x and y, are partially similar if x contains a quasi-constituent (*a*) that is similar to a quasi-constituent (*b*) contained in y (x *Ae* y). This relation is symmetric. However, it is not posited as a basic relation because it can be derived from one of its own subclasses: namely, from the relation of similarity that holds between x – *qua* chronologically prior – and y – *qua* chronologically later. This subclass constitutes, precisely, a recollection of similarity (an asymmetric relation), for a comparison between x and y is possible only if x continues to appear within a representation-recollection. The recollection of similarity is cognitively primary relative to *Ae* (this is only briefly mentioned by Carnap at the beginning of §78), and is selected, also for this reason, as a basic relation.

Starting from this basis (namely, the basis constituted by the list of pairs of lived experiences for which the relation *Er* holds), it is possible to carry out the derivation of *Ae*, of the similarity circles (relative to *Ae*), of the elementary lived experiences, of the quality classes (which indicate the single sense qualities) and of the partial equivalence of two lived experiences. Insofar as it is deemed possible to derive all scientific objects from the recollection of similarity, it is therefore to be affirmed that every statement concerning any object is, *materialiter*, a statement concerning lived experiences, and, *formaliter*, a statement concerning the recollection of similarity (§83). The constructional system can be presented by means of 'four languages' (§95) (the language of logistics, its paraphrase in word language, the realist language – which indicates the content that, in a real consciousness, corresponds to the constructed object – and the language that conjectures a consciousness containing nothing but the constructional system and expanding according to the expansion of this system). Strictly speaking, these four languages are different formulations of that *particular language* that is the constructional system itself. That is to say, this system is a linguistic construction that is developed *within* the total unity of knowledge or the total unity of language (given by scientific and ordinary knowledge). In other words, the relation between 'Language I' (the constructional system) and 'Language II' (the comprehensive unity of knowledge), which Carnap systematically studies in *The Logical Syntax of Language*, is already implicitly at work in the *Structure*. At this stage, it occurs that the constructional language, which is to construct intersubjective knowledge, necessarily presupposes a global language – namely, the (incommunicable, subjective) concreteness from which intersubjective formalisms can be abstracted.

Once again, it is necessary to take note of the projections of a few epistemic figures, characteristic of the 'systems' of romantic idealism, onto the constructional system: the choice of basis (for Fichte, as well, the value of the choice of ground for the system is given by the actual possibility of rationally reconstructing the system of knowledge), that is to say, the problem of *beginning* and of the possibility of giving an account of simple determinations; the concern directed at not letting deduced determinations contain more than has effectively been deduced (this concern is explicitly expressed in §102, in which Carnap recalls 'the mistake of not restricting to what may occur in the construction of an object'); lastly, the relation between originary consciousness (the total unity of knowledge) and the consciousness that proceeds to rationally reconstruct the originary content by progressively conforming to it, in such a way that what is 'for us' comes to be also 'for itself'. This latter relation is expressed in the *Structure* through the hypothesis of a subject A (cf. §§99 ff.) that gradually conforms to 'us', who 'know all of reality' (§102). This is to be understood not in the sense that this conforming itself rationally reconstructs the concreteness of knowledge (as it happens, for instance, in the Hegelian system), but in the sense that the formal structures realise an interaction process by means of which they come to be posited as the formal and intersubjective projection of the entirety of the system of knowledge.

In the systems of romantic idealism, on the other hand, ordinary consciousness is deduced as a necessary moment of truth (insofar as it is assumed that truth can be constituted only if consciousness has gone through the different forms of untruth); a moment, however, that needs to be included in the dialectical process. A sort of deduction of the content of ordinary consciousness (let us also include scientific consciousness in this expression) is also performed in the constructional system; in this case, however, the inclusion in the dialectical process consists only in freeing ordinary consciousness from any metaphysical bias: the *content* of ordinary consciousness, however, is retained, and constitutes, in fact, the total horizon of knowledge. 'The constructional system is a rational reconstruction of a cognitive process whose results are already known' (§102). §100 explicitly remarks upon the 'supplementations' added to experience by ordinary and scientific consciousness (namely, the supplementations that exceed the pure phenomenological content). This remark, however, does not lead, as in the case of Husserl's method, to a suspension or bracketing of the supplementations with the prospect of letting a pure phenomenological content emerge. It aims, instead, to clarify those cognitive connections (intuitively and customarily implemented within real consciousness) that the constructional system *presupposes within itself* by rationally reconstructing them; through this reconstruction, the constructional system does not refute them, but arranges them according to their relations of reducibility (cf. §126 for the construction of the unseen parts of a thing, §132 for unconscious psychological objects, §135 more generally for supplementations). Carnap does indeed accept the Husserlian notion of *epoché* (§64), to the extent that, at the beginning of the constructional system, experiences 'must simply be taken as they are given' (*ibid.*), thereby refuting the acceptance of the statements that posit the determinations of experience as being either real or unreal and illusory; the phenomenological suspension, however, is only assigned the task of clearing the basis of the system in order to be able to methodically derive from it precisely that positing of reality and unreality that had at first been bracketed, and which occurs intuitively within ordinary and scientific consciousness. That is to say, the phenomenological method is employed at the beginning of a conceptual arrangement of human knowledge that constitutes a sustained violation of that method. (This is the case regardless of the fundamental remark that *both* the phenomenological method *as well as* ordinary consciousness constitute, insofar as they are faiths in the self-evidence of the emergence from and return into nothingness, a most radical violation of the content that authentically appears.)

However, one should not lose sight of the fact that the rational reconstruction aims to perform a neutralisation of the metaphysical components (or excesses) of scientific and ordinary language, thereby leading it back within the empirical confines that constitute its 'nature' and its original pursuit – confines which are now to be elucidated. In this respect, what is assumed as material is the set of supplementations added within the domains of science and common sense: but, precisely, with the aim of considering these supplementations in an empirical, constructional and metaphysically neutral sense, rather than with respect to their metaphysical dimension. The constructional system is thus, for what concerns its content, *pre-outlined* by a pre-systematic consciousness: a remark that, incidentally, can also be referred to the Hegelian inclusion of ordinary consciousness in the dialectical process.

The neutralisation of the metaphysical components of the supplementations is due, in particular, to the principle according to which the construction of supplemented domains, 'which also contain objects which do not immediately appear within the lived experiences, does not consist in anything but an appropriate reorganisation of the objects which immediately appear' (§132). This warning applies to the construction of the unperceived parts of a thing, and is frequently repeated and clarified for the construction of other individuals' psychological domains, as well as for the constructional use of other individuals' reports (§144). The construction of what is unperceived is mainly governed by 'supplementations by analogy' (§135), which concern partially perceived processes that are supplemented in a manner analogous to that in which the corresponding total processes have been perceived in the past.

The construction of other individuals' psychological domains (which is one of the most important forms of supplementation) occurs through the attribution of one's own (my) psychological processes to the other person's body (which is already constructed *qua* physical thing), and this attribution is carried out on the basis of the observation of the other person's physical behaviour. The concept of other individuals' lived experiences – or, simply, of their experience – is formed as a result of this attribution; this concept, however, is the concept of a specific organisation of *my* lived experience and of its constituents (§140). When my experience is attributed to another person, however, it is not attributed *qua mine*, but *qua* something that is *analogous* to my actual experience. When common sense states that A is joyful, it does not – *usually* – mean to assert that A experiences precisely my feeling of joy, *qua* lived by me, but rather a feeling that is analogous to mine. ('Usually': for it is not possible to exclude instances of abnormal or infantile attitudes of ordinary consciousness, in which things go precisely the way they usually do not. Carnap, however, states that the construction aims to rationally reconstruct the normal – non-pathological, non-defective – aspects of ordinary consciousness; cf. *Structure*, Preface to the second edition.)

Therefore, in the *Structure*, the construction of other individuals' worlds is the construction of a part of my world. Let us indicate the other person by M; M's world, or M's constructional system (SM), is thereby formed as part *of the* (that is, of my) constructional system (S). There is, therefore, a certain analogy between S and SM; but even if the analogy is incomplete, or absent, it is possible to establish an intersubjective coordination between the physical and psychological world of S and the one of SM: namely, the same relations hold among the elements of the two worlds. This statement, as well, is based on other individuals' linguistic reports, and is therefore one of the many syntheses of ordinary consciousness that are reconstructed in the constructional system. Objects that are intersubjectively coordinated in the two systems form 'the same object'. Since there exists the possibility of constructing, within S, a plurality of constructional subsystems that are analogous to SM, the class of all objects that, in the different systems, are intersubjectively coordinated with an object of any of these systems is called an intersubjective object; and the world of these objects, which is the authentic object domain of science, is called an intersubjective world.

Concerning the construction of cultural objects, Carnap expresses the hope (§150) for the development of a 'logic of the cultural sciences' – which would have, first of all, to delimit these object domains, indicating those (primary) cultural objects whose construction would not require the construction of any other cultural object – and of a 'phenomenology of the cultural sciences', which would have to derive the primary cultural objects from the psychological ones (which are their indicators and manifestations). That is to say, while the construction of the physical world benefits from the advanced state of the natural sciences, the construction of the psychological and, in particular, cultural worlds must wait for psychology and for the cultural sciences to reach a sufficient scientific level. The construction of a cultural object – for instance, the 'State' – always consists, however, of a reduction of this concept: to the psychological conditions of a certain group of people; to their linguistic – and, more generally, expressive – behaviour; to the physical objects that construct that behaviour; and, therefore, to my lived experiences, which construct those physical objects according to a determinate ordering that conforms with the recollection of similarity. Once again, this does not mean, as it does for metaphysical systems, that cultural objects 'consist' of psychological ones – and that the latter consist of physical objects – for a construction simply concerns the logical relations between different kinds of objects – none excluded – that appear in experience.

Beyond science and rationality, there remains metaphysics. Realism, idealism and phenomenalism are only opposed to each other with respect to the metaphysical concept of reality; they agree for what concerns everything else, and construction theory is their shared neutral ground (§§177–178). The latter essentially consists in assuming that 'all knowledge ultimately traces back to my lived experiences, which are correlated, connected, and synthesised' (§178). Anything more that may be found in construction theory belongs to logic.

In the previous pages, it has been shown that the reasons that lead to the development of construction theory and of the constructional system disclose that an epistemic conviction is at work at the origin of the whole *Structure* – one that, through the presupposition of a plurality of subjects, claims that intersubjective agreements can be realised in relation to the formal structuring of my lived experiences. In this way, the phenomenological conception of experience (according to which construction theory and the constructional system are developed) is inscribed within a subjectivist conception of experience. And the methodological (that is, epistemically neutral) intent to construct an apparatus for the intersubjective communication of scientific knowledge comes to be compromised by an epistemic presupposition (which, incidentally, is to this day still at work within scientific research).[1]

The constructional system can be identified with the system of objectivity-intersubjectivity because the formal structure of elementary lived experiences that constitutes the construction is posited as a meaning that can be shared between a multiplicity of individuals. The possibility of different systematic organisations – relative to the one adopted in the *Structure*, which assumes as its basis my lived experiences – is already acknowledged in the *Structure* itself. In the 1961 Preface, Carnap emphasises how, in the *Structure* (§59), he has indicated 'the possibility of another system form', which would assume as its basis physical objects ('physicalism' consists precisely of this form). 'In addition to the three system forms with a basis in the physical domain, which are given in the *Structure* as examples (§62), I would now especially consider also a form that contains as basic elements physical things, and as basic concepts observable properties and observable relations of such things. One of the advantages of this basis is the fact that relative to the properties and relations of the indicated sort, there is a greater degree of intersubjective agreement [*eine grössere intersubjektive Übereinstimmung besteht*]. All concepts that scientists use in their pre-systematic linguistic communication are of this sort. Hence a constructional system with such a basis seems particularly suitable for a rational reconstruction of the conceptual system of the empirical sciences'. The will that there exist a multiplicity of subjects – which would have the formal structuring of elementary lived experiences as shared content – is equivalent to the will that there exist those conditions of consensus, without which domination is not possible (this will is not necessarily bounded, but rather tends, in the most recent stages of Western thought, to free itself from the realist-epistemic form that wills those conditions). That is to say, this will does not depend on the form that the constructional system assumes in the *Structure*, where my lived experiences constitute the basis of the system, but represents a constant throughout Carnap's investigations. The content shared by the multiplicity of subjects – a multiplicity that is willed by that will – is therefore not the intersubjective world that is constructed *as a part* of the constructional system, but it is the constructional system itself, which from the outset is constructed from *within* that will.

After the *Structure*, Carnap's enquiry has proceeded towards a constructional system whose levels are not completely reducible to elementary lived experiences by means of a series of explicit definitions, and in which increasing importance is ascribed to those scientific 'theoretical concepts' that can be put in relation to immediate and observable experiences. This, however, does not take place by means of explicit definitions formulated in terms of relations between elementary lived experiences, but only by means of 'correspondence rules' (*Zuordnungsregeln*), whereby 'theoretical concepts' receive an 'interpretation' – one which, however, always remains incomplete and an open problem. This development of the concept of construction also has repercussions for the meaning of intersubjectivity within that very system: 'At present I am inclined to think that the same holds for all concepts that refer to other individuals' psychological domains, whether they occur in scientific psychology or in everyday life' (*Structure*, Preface to the second edition). What holds for the 'theoretical concepts' of physics is then to be asserted about these concepts of intersubjectivity: namely, that they are postulates, whose content cannot be translated into statements concerning sense experiences by means of explicit definitions, but rather receive through these very experiences an 'interpretation' that always remains incomplete and an open problem. In this way, intersubjectivity, *qua* constructional concept, no longer constitutes a specific organisation of my lived experiences – one which would therefore be utterly devoid of any transcendent intentionality; rather, it converges once again, *as to its content*, towards that sense of intersubjectivity that appears in the will that wills the consensus (that is, in the will to power), within which the constructional system is developed. *As to its content*: for within this will – as developed in Carnap's enquiry – the existence of an intersubjective dimension still represents an epistemic absolute, whereas, in the new structuring of the constructional system, it appears as a theoretical postulate. In this latter case, however, this postulate is still far from being regarded as the expression of a will that not only wills the domination of the world, but also wills and imposes the very meaning of domination (according to what has been said in paragraph XXI ff. of Part I of the present volume). The 'theoretical concepts' – and, therefore, the postulate of intersubjectivity – are 'interpreted' from sense experience in the same way in which a formal system is interpreted by attributing determinate values to its variables. The will that wills the consensus, on the other hand, *interprets* sense experience in such a way that the very existence of domination is not a given or a datum, produced by scientific practice, but is rather the outcome of an interpreting will – which, precisely, does not 'find' that a certain configuration of the given or of the datum constitutes domination, but *wills* it.

Notes

Emanuele Severino: Beyond the alienated soul of tradition and contemporary philosophical thought

1   The Accademia dei Lincei (Lincean Academy) is one of the most important academies in the world. Founded in 1603, Galileo Galilei was once among its members. The academy closed in 1651 and reopened in the 1870s to become the national academy of Italy, encompassing both literature and science among its concerns.

2   E. Severino. *La struttura originaria* [*The Originary Structure*], Brescia: La Scuola, 1958; new edition, with changes and an introduction, Milan: Adelphi, 1981. E. Severino. *Essenza del nichilismo*, Brescia: Paideia, 1972; second edition, Milan: Adelphi, 1982; Engl. transl. *The Essence of Nihilism*, New York, London: Verso, 2016.

3   R. Carnap. *La costruzione logica del mondo. Pseudo-problemi nella filosofia* [*The Logical Structure of the World: Pseudoproblems in Philosophy*], ed. and trans. by E. Severino, Milan: Fabbri, 1966; new edition, Torino: Utet, 1997.

4   E. Severino, *La struttura originaria* [*The Originary Structure*], Introduction.

5   E. Severino, *The Essence of Nihilism*, p. 69.

The unity of knowledge

1   Cf. Part I: 'Law and Chance' in this volume, as well as E. Severino, *Studi di filosofia della prassi*, Milan: Adelphi, 1984, Part I, Chap. III.

The protocol-statement debate

1   About the 'protocol-statement debate' cf. the introduction and commentary to *Über das Fundament der Erkenntnis* (*Sul fondamento della conoscenza*, ed. by E. Severino, Brescia: La Scuola, 1963). About the 'verification principle' cf. *Studi di filosofia della prassi*, Part III, Chap. I (paragraph 1), Chap. II.

The presupposition of intersubjectivity in *the logical structure of the world*

1   Translator's note: Quotations from the *Structure* have been adapted in order to conform with Severino's own translation of Carnap's text. R. Carnap, *The Logical Structure of the World and Pseudoproblems in Philosophy*, trans. by R.A. George, Berkeley, CA: University of California Press, 1969.

2   Translator's note: 'The series of experiences is different for each subject'.

3   M. Schlick, '*Erleben, Erkennen, Metaphysik*', in *Gesammelte Aufsätze*, Vienna: Gerold, 1938, pp. 1 ff (*Kant-Studien*, 31, 1926, pp. 146–158).

4   *ibid.*, p. 2.

Intersubjective knowledge *qua* structural knowledge

1 Translator's note: 'Logistics' refers to the German '*Logistik*'.

The concept of construction

1 Translator's note: 'cultural' translates the German '*geistig*'.

Realist language formulation of the concept of construction

1 Translator's note: 'notion' translates here Aristotle's *nóema*.

The method of quasi-analysis: Goodman's critical observations

1 The original text (§70) mentions a series of *five* colours: this is the only change that we make for greater simplicity and clarity.

2 All of these remarks by Goodman are correct – according to the notion of correctness of the empirical-scientific standpoint: that is, according to a hypothetical correctness. One might ask what guarantee is given for the statement that a certain pair is not included in a certain list of pairs: namely, on what ground is the possibility excluded that, going through the list again (however short it may be), a pair that was absent should not come to be found within the list? Or vice-versa? These questions are part of a broader critical remark, according to which

every enumeration of empirical objects remains, in spite of all precautions, merely a hypothesis. Here, however, we find ourselves in a situation in which, by adopting certain operational presuppositions, the construction of intersubjective knowledge is attempted. This attempt clashes against certain difficulties that render the communication of knowledge ambiguous; some of these difficulties have been indicated by Goodman.

In the pages that we have considered, however, Goodman never refers to the question of intersubjectivity – disregarding which, one would come to lose track of the authentic reasons that led to the development of the method of quasi-analysis in the *Structure*. (However, the construction theory and the constructional system advanced by Goodman still remain within the confines of the question of intersubjectivity, in spite of the clarifications, amendments and – even substantial – critiques that he addresses to the *Structure*: the constructions proposed by Goodman aim to be 'quite as intersubjective as those of any other system'; Goodman, *The Structure of Appearance*, p. 107.) That is to say, Goodman does not go beyond the formal reason (to which we have already referred earlier) indicated in §68 of the *Structure*: namely, that the fundamental elements of a system are to be treated, within that same system, as unanalysable units. For Goodman, this is a 'triviality' (*ibid.*, p. 118). Nevertheless, the unanalysability of lived experiences is completely *sui generis*: namely, it indicates – let us reiterate – the impossibility of transferring the concrete qualities of experience into linguistic analysis. Experience, intact and unanalysed, remains outside of language: not in the sense that *perception*, in not recognising the multiplicity and compositeness of experience, does not analyse it (so much so that each lived experience is posited as the totality of qualities present at a certain instant of the temporal process), but in the sense that *communication* – intersubjective knowledge – cannot rely on perception. That is to say, it cannot rely on the way in which experience is analysed by perception, but must rather rely on a linguistic projection of experience. The latter, even if it is not able to reproduce the qualitative concreteness of experience, is however able to structurally define it by indicating the networks of relations that hold for each lived experience – and therefore by constructing a *sui generis* kind of analysis.

On the other hand, the argument of the *Structure* becomes inexplicably arbitrary if one simply considers, as Goodman does, the rationale of the unanalysability of experiences indicated in §68. If isolated from its context, the assertion – according to which classes and relations of experiences, as well as classes and relations of those classes and relations, constitute a synthetic procedure – clashes at least with the thesis of construction theory, according to which a class is equivalent to what its elements have in common (§33). Each lived experience, insofar as it is an element of multiple classes, is subjected to an actual and proper analytic procedure, and the ground of its unanalysability comes in this way to disappear. By considering, on the other hand, the extensional character of classes and relations – and by considering that extensional procedures are supposed to realise that formal treatment of experience that, by letting go of the qualitative aspect of experience and of the psychological meaning of the statements that express it, affords the construction of intersubjective knowledge – the non-analytic character of these procedures becomes apparent. At the same time, however, it also becomes apparent that this lack of analysis characterises intersubjective language *relative to* the analysis to which the single lived experience is subjected in the act of perception.

A reading of §71 also confirms that analysis is cast aside only *relative to* the level of communication (and that, therefore, quasi-analysis is the specific trait of intersubjective knowledge). In the 'example', it is stated that the sound *c - e - g*, 'according to its phenomenal manifestation, namely, according to its perceivable givenness', is a unitary totality (whence it can appear – erroneously, however – that the argument aims to cast analysis aside on the level of perception, rather than on that of intersubjectivity). Right after, it is nevertheless acknowledged that the sound *c - e - g* has a tone kinship with all sounds containing *c*, as well as with all sounds containing *e* or *g*, and that it therefore belongs to three classes of sounds. The perception of this kinship, however, is possible *only* if *c - e - g* is perceived *as a difference* (a unified difference, clearly, but a unity of difference), rather than as a simple meaning: otherwise, every ground for asserting that it has a kinship with sounds differing from one another would come to disappear. Perceiving *c - e - g* as a difference means, however, properly analysing it. This is the case even if it is held (as noted in the 'example' of §71) that the perception of difference is realised only in correlation to the perception of sounds akin to c - e - g: this remark does not cast the existence of analysis aside, but rather indicates the conditions of its realisation.

What is, then, the meaning of the text's insistence on denying that c - e - g has any parts, that it is composed of constituents, etc.? *Once it is retained that the perception of difference is the condition of the perception of a tone kinship with other sounds* (in the same way in which, as it were, the perception of kinship is a condition of the perception of the internal differentiation of c - e - g), that insistence can only aim to exclude that the parts of c - e - g are separate things and that each is perceived independently of the others. Carnap attempts then to deduce the statement of the separation of the parts by positing it as a consequence of an unintentional application of quasi-analysis. Indeed, the construction of similarity circles, already intuitively carried out by ordinary consciousness – and, therefore, following the example, the construction of the similarity circles c, e, g – gives the impression that c, e, g are three autonomous parts, of which c - e - g would be the sum; whereas, in fact, they are 'three different directions' in which it is possible to proceed starting from the unitary sound. That is to say, they are, indeed, three parts (for, otherwise, there would be no ground for proceeding from the unitary sound precisely in those three directions, rather than in any others), but they are not abstractly separate parts or members of a mere collection. And in §36 (which can be conveniently applied here), it is asserted that 'it is likely that there are no mere collections at all', and that every whole is a system.

This does not get rid of the impression that the text cannot adequately control the distinction between the perceptual unanalysability of lived experiences (i.e. excluding that these are composed of autonomous and separate parts) and the unanalysability of experiences on the level of intersubjective communication. It is clear, however, that quasi-analysis, which leads to intersubjective definitions, can construct relation descriptions only on the (subjective) basis of a perceptual analysis of lived experience. And it is also clear that, in intersubjective definitions, the unanalysability of lived experiences entails that language does not make use of their qualitative composition, but rather of their being 'orderly placed in several kinship contexts on the basis of a kinship relation' (§71): 'Scientific statements speak of pure forms [namely, of the formal properties of relations], without stating what the elements and the relations of these forms are' (§12). Indeed, if in the 'examples' of §70 and §71 it is a kinship relation of colour or tone that is discussed, it must be kept in mind that, in intersubjective definitions, the psychological meaning of this relation is not expressed, and only its formal property – namely, its 'structure', and, in this case, its being a reflexive and symmetric relation – is retained.

Scientific-ordinary knowledge and constructional systems

1   It would be incorrect to claim that this presupposition re-emerges in the last part of the *Structure* ('Clarification of Some Philosophical Problems on the Basis of Construction Theory'), which instead contains commendable analyses of a phenomenological-constructional character, such as the one concerning the difference between individual and general concepts (§158), the ones concerning identity (§159), the 'I' (§163), causality (§165), and the psychophysical relation (§§166, 168). After having excluded the metaphysical concept of reality from the constructional system (insofar as this concept is independent of consciousness), Carnap acknowledges that construction theory and realism agree, among other things, on the notion that real empirical objects 'are independent of their being cognised, in the sense that they also exist at times when they do not appear in my (or someone else's) lived experiences' (§177). This statement, together with similar ones, is to be understood while keeping in mind the metaphysically neutral meaning that they come to assume once the supplementations of experience are regarded as a specific organisation of experience itself. According to the stance of realism, the concept of independence from consciousness aims to have a transcendent intentionality, and it is, therefore, a metaphysical concept; this very same concept, however, becomes an empirico-constructional one if it is regarded as a coordination of experiences.

Index

Note: References followed by "n" refer to endnotes.

absoluteness 26
absolute value 75, 76
abyssal alienation 59
Accademia dei Lincei 157n1
alienation 59–60
analogical reasoning 112
analytic proposition 45
anti-absolutism 76
antinomic character of
        immutables 10, 11, 17
antinomicity 65
antinomy 10, 11
a posteriori matter 143
a priori synthesis 26, 44, 45, 143
Aristotle 14, 16, 63, 80
Ars conjectandi (Bernoulllli) 40
Artaud, Antonin 19
attestation 65, 66
autómaton 15
available outcomes 42, 43
axiomatic/axiom(atisation)
    of convergence 46
    of disorder 46

    of geometry 93–4
    structures 95

Bakunin, Mikhail 34
becoming of all things 11–12
becoming of world 6, 10, 17
    absolute unpredictability of 6,
        47
    domination of 11, 13, 21
    existence of 18
    experience of 5
    Greek meaning of 11–12,
        19–20, 22, 35
    stream 92
    vision of 11
Begriffsschrift 39
'being-mine' ('*l'esser mia*') of
        experience 72
being-nothing (*esser niente*) 12, 51
Beobachtungsaussagen 77
Beobachtungssätze 77
Bernoulllli, Daniel 40
Bohr, Niels 49, 52

calculus 39, 46
Carnap, Rudolf 33, 87, 99, 104,
    131, 134, 139–41, 144, 153
  accepting Husserlian notion of
    epoché 148
  agreeing construction theory
    and realism 163n1
  class of objects 94
  on confirmability of statement
    114, 116–17
  constructional system 119
  construction theory 95
  corrections to *Structure* 93
  definition of intersubjectivity
    111
  enquiry towards
    constructional system
    154–6
  Gegenstandsvorstellungen 109
  permissibility of argument
    101–3
  philosophical work of 79–80
  physical language *qua*
    universal language of
    science 96
  presentation 86
  and presupposition 92–3
  procedures of science and
    common sense 112
  radical approach of
    Pseudoproblems 113
  about reality 107
  remarks about lived
    experiences 124
  statement and proposition 100
  studies in constructional
    language 146–7

systematisations of knowledge
    96–7
  verification method 108
  views on ordinary
    consciousness 150
chance 14–15, 29, 47–8
  forms or outcomes of 27
  fundamental problem of
    theory of 46
choice 128, 146
civilisation of technics (*civiltà
    della tecnica*) 4
classes and relations 102–3, 129,
    136–42, 161n2
cognitively primary relative 128
  to lived experiences 143
  to matter 144
cognitive primacy 119–20, 128
  order of objects in
    systematisation 122
  relationship with object types
    120–2
  theory of 124
cognitive value 120
collectives 26–7, 44
communication 135, 160n2
  intersubjective 123, 136,
    153
  pre-systematic linguistic 154,
    162n2
confirmability of statement 114,
    116–17
confirmation of trial 22–3, 24–6
consciousness
  ordinary 147–50
  pre-systematic 149
  scientific 147, 148, 149

constructed statements, sense of 120

constructional system(atisation) (*Konstitutionssystem*) 95, 99, 103, 113, 119–21, 147–8
   basic elements 143–5, 154
   choice of basis 146
   constructional arrangements of objects 124
   constructional essence 123
   of cultural objects 151–2
   development within subjectivist perspective 125
   epistemic absoluteness 156
   epistemic conviction 153
   extensional statements of 133
   languages 145–6
   multiplicity of subjects 154
   neutralisation of metaphysical components 149–50
   with objectivity-intersubjectivity system 153
   of other individuals' psychological domains 150–1
   phenomenological suspension 148–9
   rational reconstruction 149
   reality of plurality of subjects 124–5
   systems of romantic idealism 146–7
   of transcendent intentionality 122, 155
construction of object 99–100, 102, 105–6
   classes and relations 102, 103
   intensional statements 104
   propositional functions 101–2, 103
construction of similarity circles 162n2
construction theory (*Konstitutionstheorie*) 95, 113
contemplation 9
contents of consciousness (*in den Erlebnisinhalten*) 91
continuum 23
cosmogenic circle 7
cultural objects 100, 121
   construction of 151–2
   reduction to physical objects 122
cultural operation 38

data/datum (*dato*) 12, 31–2, 35, 56
   absolute character 35, 36
   additional meaning 54, 55
   affording structure of predictions 32
   of experience 55
   formalisms 39
   and interpretation 53–4
   intersubjective and linguistic character 33
   intersubjective consensus 34, 35–6
   moral law and epistemic concept 35
   protocol statements 33–4
   social 55
Descartes, René 63, 64

determinism 49
    destruction of 48, 52
    refutation of 48
dialogic relation 86
*Die Reihe der Erlebnisse ist für
    jedes Subjekt verschieden*
    80
Dietzgen, Joseph 34
domination of becoming 3, 6, 11,
    13, 21. *See also* modern
    science; science
    existence of becoming 18
    forms of 10, 11, 22
    sequence of events 15
    will to power 53, 57

elementary lived experiences
    127–8. *See also* lived
    experiences
    derivation of similarity circles
    145
    formal structure of 153, 154
    ordered system of relations
    129–30
    quasi-analysis 130–1
    as 'unanalysable units' 129
empirical regularity 24–5
epistéme 4, 8, 10, 21, 28, 53
    absolute value 75, 76
    characteristic traits 31
    contradiction of 26
    domination of becoming 11,
    13
    immutable being of 9–10
    immutables of 29
    synthetic *a priori* principle 40
    verification principle 68

epistemic absoluteness 156
epistemic prediction 8, 10, 25, 35,
    36
epoché 124, 148
'equally likely' ('*equipossibili*')
    events 41
Erkennen (conceptual knowledge)
    81
Erleben (immediate lived
    experience) 81, 82
Erleben, Erkennen, Metaphysik
    (Schlick) 81
Erlebnisse (lived experiences) 80,
    82
eternal beings 7–10
existence
    of becoming 18
    true dimension of 35
    views among scientific
    researchers and
    philosophers 64
existentialism 71
Experience, Cognition and
    Metaphysics. *See Erleben,
    Erkennen, Metaphysik*
    (Schlick)
experience(s) 21, 22, 68, 127. *See
    also* lived experiences
    atomic constituents of 127
    of becoming 50
    being-mine of 72
    data/datum of 31–2, 55
    empirical 99
    linguistic projection of 160n2
    meaningfulness of concept of
    71–2
    nonsubjectivist notion of 125

phenomenological conception of 153
philosophical and methodological significance 77–8
philosophical conception of 87–8
reference to 65
structure of 129, 144
unity of 71
extension
of coextensive functions 105
of propositional function 102
of relations 113
statements 103

fact 65, 76
false proposition 101–2
favourable outcomes 41–3
Fichte, Johann Gottlieb 146
flowing stratification (*stratificazione fluente*) 128
formal axiomatic systems 37
destruction of the immutables 38
non-contradictory nature of 37
theoretical apparatus of logico-mathematical formalisms 37–8
formalisms 39, 135
intersubjective 93, 146
logico-mathematical 11, 38, 39
pure 92, 94–5
formaliter 145
Frege, G. 39, 100, 103, 104
frequency hypothesis 46

Galilei, Galileo 157n1
Gegenstandsvorstellung 116, 117
Gegenstandsvorstellungen 109
Gestaltpsychologie 128
gígnesthai apó túches 14–15
Gödel, Kurt Friedrich 37–8
Goodman, Nelson 139, 141, 159–61n2

Hegel, Georg Wilhelm Friedrich 65, 95
Heisenberg, Werner 49, 52
Hilbert, David 37, 39, 93
Humean critique of inductive process 25
Husserl, Edmund 111, 124, 148
hypothetical prediction 22, 57

idealism 71, 152
immutable(s) 15–16, 36
antinomic character of 17
being of *epistéme* 9–10
destruction of 19–20, 21, 35, 38
of *epistéme* 29
and eternal beings 7, 9, 10
impossibility of 20
invocation of 18
law of 17
meaning of existence introduced by 16
order 7, 8
independence, concept of 163n1
indeterminacy
of momentum 51–2
of position of particle 51
principle of 48–9

indeterminism 27. *See also* determinism

indicators
  of objects 106, 107, 119
  of other individuals' psychological processes 111
  of physical objects 122
  of psychological dimension 112

indifference states, principle of 41, 42
  analytic character of 42–3
  classical theory of probability 42–4
  epistemic character of 45

individual empirical object 100

inductive inference 47

intensional statements 104

intentionality 111
  real 114
  transcendent 117, 122, 155, 163

interpretation 53, 155
  non-subjectivist 49
  social consensus 55–6
  will to power as 53–4

intersubjective agreement 64, 75, 92

intersubjective communication 136

intersubjective consciousness 83

intersubjective consensus 34, 35–6, 39

intersubjective knowledge 66, 87, 160n2
  construction of 76, 160n2

determinating relation among linguistic conducts 69
  sign system of 70
  techniques for construction of 71
  unitary systematisation of 67, 68

'intersubjectively transferrable' relations 92

intersubjective objects 151

intersubjective science, construction of 88

intersubjective world 151

intersubjectivity 91, 144
  Carnap's definition of 111
  development 111–12
  implicit identification of 80–1
  physical language 96
  presupposition of intersubjectivity 81–3
  pure formalism 94–5
  reference to experience 65
  for rejection of metaphysics 64
  Wittgenstein and Schlick's neopositivist concept 111

intuition, absolute character/value of 36–7

intuitive meanings, absolute character of 36–7

irruption
  of becoming 13, 15
  of unforeseen, possibility of 23
  of unpredictable social event 38

Kant, Immanuel 64, 65, 109, 144

kat'exochén' 83

Keynes, John Maynard 38
knowledge 3–4, 81, 83, 94, 107. *See*
    also intersubjective
    knowledge; scientific
    knowledge
  entirety of 100
  metaphysical 114
  objective-intersubjective 104
  positivist unification of 63
  scientific 23
  synthetic *a priori* 25
  unitary systematisation of
    63–4, 66

language 68, 78, 86, 87, 100, 146
  constructional 113, 145–6
  construction in realist
    presupposition 113
  extensional 104, 114
  intensional 104
  intersubjective 32, 70, 77, 96,
    161n2
  logistic 93, 145
  neo-positivist/neo-positivism
    to 52, 66
  physical 96
  problem of structure of 69
  realist 106–7, 145
  reference to empirical
    experiences 70
  scientific character of 114
law 47–8
  of formation 45
  of immutables 17
  moral 35
  and nothingness 16–17
  probabilistic 50

Lincean Academy. *See* Accademia
    dei Lincei
linguistic conduct 68, 69, 72–3,
    87
linguistic construction 146
link descriptions 133, 134
lived experiences 88, 124, 143. *See*
    also experience(s)
  cognitively primary relative to
    143
  stream of 92, 127, 128
  unanalysability of 160n2,
    161n2, 162n2
  unity-totality of 128
Logical Structure of the World, The
    (Carnap) 79–81, 85, 103,
    104, 111, 119
  aim of 115
  Carnap's corrections to 93,
    95–6
  constructional language 146
  constructional systematisation
    120, 121
  construction of other
    individuals' worlds in 151
  elementary lived experiences
    as 'unanalysable units'
    129
  epistemic conviction 153
  language construction 113
  meaninglessness in 110
  meaning of object-names
    85–7
  order of objects in
    systematisation 122
  physicalism 87
  process of emancipation 96

recollection of similarity 144
structures of relations 88–9
systematisation 96–7
Logical Syntax of Language, The
(Carnap) 93, 96, 104, 114
constructional language 146
logical value 105, 108, 116, 120,
123
logico-mathematical formalisms
scientific character of
theoretical construction
39
theoretical apparatus of 37–8

Marxism 38, 124
materialiter 145
meaningfulness
of concept of experiences
71–2
of scientific statement 85
meaninglessness 69, 110
meaningless expression 50
neo-positivist concept of 52
meta-empirical character 69
metaphysical/metaphysics 18, 152,
163
knowledge 114
neo-positivist critique of 115
repudiation of 64
modern science 4–5, 21, 48, 93
datum in 32
scientific rationality 29
transformation of causal laws
27
will to power 53
momentum, indeterminacy of
51–2

neocapitalism 38
neo-positivism 64, 66, 67, 112,
114–15
harmony with ample divisions
of contemporary
philosophy 71
philosophical stance of 68–9
procedures of science and
common sense 112
protocol-statement debate
76–8
radical identification of order
of rationality 70
shortcomings of 67–8
verification principle 68,
69
Neurath, Otto 33, 75, 77, 96
neutrality 67, 124
non-nothingness (*un non-niente*)
46. *See also* nothingness
not-being-any of things 13
nothingness 11–13, 15
events 24
Greek meaning of 13–14
issues from 51
law and 16–17
meaningless expression 50
neo-positivist concept of
meaninglessness 52
transformation to non-
nothingness 46
unpredictablility of 25–6

object-names, meaning of
85–6
by characterisation 86–7
by presentation 86

objectivity 91, 92, 94, 95
  objective-intersubjective
    knowledge 104
  objective-intersubjective
    structure of reality 109
  objectivity-intersubjectivity
    93
  objectivity-intersubjectivity
    system 153
object(s) 151. *See also*
    construction of object;
    cultural objects; physical
    objects; psychological
    objects
  cognitive order of 97
  constructional arrangements
    of 124
  designation of 89
  domains 100
  indicators of 106, 107–8, 119
  intersubjective 151
  sphere 101
  structural characterisation of
    93–4
  of vision 5

'partial similarity' relation (*Ae*)
    144–5
particle
  indeterminacy of position of
    51
  indeterminate position or
    velocity 52
  subsequent state of 50–1
perception of kinship 160–2n2
permissibility of argument 101–2
phenomenalism 152

phenomenological/
    phenomenology 71
  principle 76
  suspension 124, 148–9
philosophical-metaphysical-
    theological horizon 63
philosophy 107, 112
  birth of 8
  death of 4
  of Hegelian kind 121
  intention of 9
  qua epistéme 17
phúsis 18
physicalism 153
physical language 96
physical objects 100, 121
  construction of 152
  indicators of 122
  possibility of reduction 144
  reduction to psychological
    objects 122
physical system, state of 27–8
Planck's constant 38
Plato 80
Popper, Karl 33, 46
positivism 63–4. *See also*
    neo-positivism
positivist unification of
    knowledge 63
power (*potenza*) 4
praxis 9, 56
prediction(s) (*previsione*) 5, 6, 7, 8
  epistemic 25
  hypothetical 22, 57
  probability of 23
  scientific 28, 36
  value of 21

presupposition 107
  of absolute value of
    extensional languages 114
  of intersubjectivity 81–3
  of plurality of subjects 153
  rationalist 91–2
  of science and common sense
    112
probabilistic/probability 39–40
  classical theory of 42–3
  distribution 47
  frequentist theory of 26
  law 50
  of prediction 23
  theory of 47
property descriptions 88, 134
proposition 100, 101, 108
  false 101–2
propositional functions 101, 105,
  108
  extension of 102–3
  permissible arguments of
    101–2, 123
  transformation of 106
protocol-statement debate 76–8
protocol statements 33–4, 75–6
pseudo-problems 109
Pseudoproblems in Philosophy
  (Carnap) 106, 109–10
  anti-metaphysical stance of 116
  language construction 113
pseudo-statements 109
psychological-subjective value 120
psychological objects 100, 121
  construction of 152
  reduction to physical objects
    122

quantum physics 47, 48, 52
quasi-analysis 130, 133, 160–2
quasi-ingredients 134
quasi-objects 101, 102, 103

rational-theoretical order 67
rationalist presupposition 91–2
rational reconstruction 105
realist/realism 152
  language 106
  presupposition 112, 113
recollection of similarity (*Er*) 144,
  145
reference
  of language to empirical
    experiences 70
  of sign 104
  of statements 105
refutation of determinism 48
Reichenbach, Hans 23, 33, 51
Reininger, Robert 33
relation
  among linguistic conducts
    69
  classes and 102–3, 129, 136–42,
    161n2
  of colour kinship 135–7, 139,
    163n2
  descriptions 88, 133, 134
  dialogic 86
  extension of 113
  'intersubjectively transferrable'
    92
  network of 134
  ordered system of 129–30
repudiation of metaphysics 64
rigour 67

romantic idealism, systems of 146–7
Russell, Bertrand 92, 93, 100, 102

Sachverhaltsvorstellung 116
Sachverhaltsvorstellungen 109
Scheler, Max 34
Schlick, M. 33, 34, 49, 81–3, 77, 87, 108, 112
Schumpeter, Joseph 38
science 3–4, 5, 7, 22, 29, 91. *See also* modern science
    axiomatisation of geometry 93–4
    experimental character of 21
    as intersubjective language 32
    success and domination of 56–7
    will to power 56
scientific inductions 27, 35
scientific knowledge 23
    intersubjective content of 129
    systematisation/systematicity of 99, 100
set, intuitive absolute character of 37
sign, sense of 104
singular ambivalence 70
social consensus 32, 34, 55–6
Sombart, Werner 34
spatio-temporal data 33
statement 100
    confirmability of 114, 116–17
    extension 103
    formulation of 109–10
    intensional 104
    and proposition 100
    protocol 33–4, 75–6
    pseudo-statements 109
    qua empirical sign 100
    reference of 105
    translatability of 123
statistical sequence 45
stream (*die Strom*) 92, 94
    of lived experiences 127, 128
Structure. See Logical Structure of the World, The (Carnap)
structure 89, 93, 94
    axiomatic 95
    descriptions 88
    of experience 129, 144
    logical 92
Structure of Appearance, The (Goodman) 139
subjective representations 104, 108–9
supplementations 148, 149
    by analogy 150
    construction of other individuals' psychological domains 150
    neutralisation of metaphysical components 149–50
synthetic *a priori* law/principle 40, 41, 44, 45
systematic complementarity 65
systematisation/systematicity of scientific knowledge 99

theoretical concepts 155, 156
theoría 9

thinking 59, 85, 86
    philosophical 65
Tractatus (Wittgenstein) 128
transcendent intentionality 117,
        122, 155, 163
translatability of statements
        123

unanalysable units 129, 130,
        133
uniform linguistic reactions 70
unitary systematisation of
        knowledge 63–4, 66
unitary totality 161n2
unity of experience 71
universality, implicit identification
        of 80–1
unsaturated signs 100

verification principle 68, 69, 108,
        116

vision (*visione*) 5, 9
    of becoming of world 11
    objects of 5
von Mises, Ludwig 26, 46

Weber, Max 38, 124
Whitehead, Alfred North 92
will to anticipate (*ante-capere*) 6
will to dominate becoming 11
will to power 19, 53
    abyssal alienation 59
    embodied by science 57
    essential alienation 59–60
    as interpretation 53–4
    originary form of 58–9
    rigour 67
    stages of 126–7
Wittgenstein, Ludwig 33, 103, 108,
        112, 128
    mistake in *Structure* 95–6
    solipsism 70–1